Earth Science Week 2020: Earth Materials in Our Lives

October 11–17, 2020
Highlights Report

American Geosciences Institute
4220 King Street
Alexandria, VA 22302 U.S.A.
www.americangeosciences.org
703-379-2480

If you have comments concerning this report, please contact:
Ed Robeck, Ph.D.
Director of Education and Outreach
American Geosciences Institute
703-379-2480 x245
ecrobeck@americangeosciences.org

See Our News Coverage

Because of the large and increasing number of news clippings citing Earth Science Week activities and resources, the print edition of the print report no longer includes clippings. To view the hundreds of press releases and news items promoting awareness of Earth Science Week each year, please visit online at **www.earthsciweek.org/highlights**. Thank you for helping us in our efforts to conserve resources and protect the environment.

Contents

Front cover: 2020 ESW poster design: AGI/Brenna Tobler.

Highlights Report: Earth Science Week 2020

The 2020 Earth Science Week Photography Contest winning entry by Alex Xu

Introduction

Held October 11–17, 2020, the 23rd annual **Earth Science Week** celebrated the theme of **"Earth Materials in Our Lives."** The 2020 event focused on the ways that Earth materials impact humans — and the ways human activity impacts these materials — in the 21st century. The Earth system includes rock, fluid, gaseous, and mineral materials that individuals and societies use to live and thrive. The availability of raw materials such as metals, aggregates, and fossil fuels influences and is influenced by human activities such as manufacturing, industry, transportation, food production, energy generation, and product recycling.

AGI organizes Earth Science Week as a service to member societies, with generous help from partners that provide funding, donate materials, organize events, and publicize the event. Funding partners in 2020 included:

- U.S. Geological Survey (USGS);
- National Park Service;
- National Aeronautics and Space Administration (NASA);
- American Geophysical Union (AGU);
- Geothermal Resources Council;
- IF/THEN® (Lyda Hill Philanthropies);
- Society for Mining, Metallurgy and Exploration (SME);
- Society of Exploration Geophysicists;
- AmericaView;
- Geological Society of America (GSA);
- Consumer Energy Alliance;
- Water Footprint Calculator (Grace Communications Foundation);
- American Meteorological Society; and
- CLEAN (Climate Literacy and Energy Awareness Network).

In addition, Earth Science Week 2020 welcomed four Global Sponsors:

- American Association of Petroleum Geologists (AAPG) Foundation;
- ExxonMobil;
- International Raw Materials Observatory; and
- Newmont Corporation.

Despite challenges arising from the global pandemic of 2020, Earth Science Week **participation remained strong.** People in all 50 states and 28 countries participated in events and activities. The Earth Science Week website received more than 494,000 page views in 2020. In addition, 123 people across the country and around the globe actively participated in the program's visual arts, video, essay, and photography contests.

Earth Science Week events, which normally include educators teaching Earth science activities in their classrooms and public outreach events in settings like parks, museums, and science centers, were more concentrated online this year, due to the pandemic. Still, participants were active in 2020. A detailed list of events can be found in the second half of this report. This list represents only events reported directly to and discovered by AGI, so please notify Earth Science Week staff if your participation is not listed.

Events also are highlighted on the Earth Science Week website (**www.earthsciweek.org/highlights**), which features press releases and other items by members of the geoscience community, as well as news media promoting Earth Science Week. Television and radio news programs covered Earth Science Week on local stations in several states. Each year, Earth Science Week media in web, print, and broadcast media coverage, along with direct outreach by AGI, reach thousands of people through hundreds of organizations in the U.S. and more than 20 countries.

This report is designed to give an overview of the activities organized by AGI and other groups for Earth Science Week. We hope this information on 2020 events and publicity inspires you to develop your own activities next year. Please visit **www.earthsciweek.org** for event planning, materials, resources, and support. Contact Earth Science Week staff at **info@earthsciweek.org** for assistance in planning for Earth Science Week.

Because of the large number of news clippings citing Earth Science Week activities and resources, the print edition of this report does not include such clips. To view the hundreds of press releases and news items promoting awareness of Earth Science Week each year, please visit online at **www.earthsciweek.org/highlights.** Thank you for helping us in our efforts to build geoscience awareness, conserve resources, and protect the environment.

Summary of Activities

Ella Giguere's finalist entry for the 2020 ESW Photography Contest

Key Partnerships and Efforts

Earth Science Week's success depends on the collaboration of key partners. In 2020, AGI pursued signature initiatives and forged partnerships with numerous organizations (listed alphabetically):

Educators seeking teaching resources and other support were directed by AGI to the **American Association of Petroleum Geologists** (AAPG) and the AAPG Foundation, both longtime supporters of Earth Science Week. In addition, Earth Science Week promoted awareness of AAPG's Distinguished Lecturer and Teacher of the Year programs. AAPG student chapters received kits. Earth Science Week participants learned about AAPG's Distinguished Lecture Series. Program participants were encouraged to participate in AAPG's Annual Convention and Exhibition. AAPG's "Modeling an Oil Reserve" activity was featured in the Earth Science Week 2020 activity calendar. Subscribers to AAPG Explorer received copies of the Earth Science Week 2020 poster in the magazine. The AAPG Foundation supported a range of Earth Science Week 2020 as a Global Sponsor.

The **American Geophysical Union** (AGU) continued its role as a supporting program partner in 2020 with the contribution of funds as well as expertise. The educator kit included an AGU poster celebrating the 50th anniversary of Earth Day and showing geoscientists' contributions to environmental stewardship. Earth Science Week's 2020 activity calendar featured AGU's "Soil, Sand, and Gravel" classroom activity. AGU's annual meetings, professional development workshops, programs for college students, print and electronic resources, and GIFT workshops were promoted through the Earth Science Week e-newsletter, website, and activity calendar.

Earth Science Week 2020 promoted awareness of the **American Institute of Professional Geologists** (AIPG), an AGI member society that advocates for geologists and certifies their credentials. AIPG offers several PowerPoint presentations online for free download, presenting career information for young, newly graduated geoscientists. AIPG also provided a geologic-timescale bookmark for the educator kit.

The **American Meteorological Society** (AMS) promoted two teacher professional development programs focusing on the atmosphere and oceans. Project Atmosphere offered comprehensive teacher professional development program based on studies in the atmospheric sciences. Project Ocean provided teacher professional development focusing on studies of the physical foundations of oceanography. In addition, AMS promoted its DataStreme professional development courses in weather, ocean, and climate science. AMS also provided a bookmark for the educator kit, connecting program participants with information about K–12 teacher professional development and related resources.

AmericaView, a longtime Earth Science Week partner, provided a two-piece "Factory Earth" poster and game for the 2020 educator kit. Supported by USGS and NASA, this material offered an education and fun way for young people and others to explore topics including Earth materials, Landsat satellites, and Earth Observation Day. Earth Observation Day, established by AmericaView, is a major part of Earth Science Week.

The **Archaeological Institute of America** (AIA), a continuing Earth Science Week partner, promoted awareness of and participation in AIA's International Archaeology Day, which takes place annually on the final day of Earth Science Week.

For the Earth Science Week 2020 Toolkit, the **Association for Women Geoscientists** provided a postcard featuring links to informational videos on groundbreaking women in geoscience history.

Earth Science Week directed participants' attention to the **Association of American Geographers** (AAG), an AGI member society that offers an array of web resources for K–12 and college-level instruction. For example, AAG's Center for Global Geography Education offers online modules for undergraduate courses in geography and related social and environmental sciences. GeoSTART helps middle- and high-school students develop geography, Earth science, and spatial thinking skills using NASA Earth Observing Missions remote sensing imagery and related data.

The **Association of American State Geologists** partnered with AGI and the USGS to support Geologic Map Day during Earth Science Week 2020. State geologists nationwide made geologic maps of their states available on their websites for students and others to use in learning activities on Geologic Map Day.

Program participants learned about resources offered by the **Association of Environmental and Engineering Geologists** (AEG). Resources include publications, section and chapter meetings, and special educator sessions at the AEG annual meeting. Opportunities for professional geologists to speak to classes are also available, as well as resume writing workshops and scholarships for students.

Earth Science Week promoted awareness of a website of great value to educators, AGI's **Center for Geoscience & Society.** Largely through its Education GeoSource database, the center enhances geoscience awareness across all sectors of society by generating new approaches to building geoscience knowledge, engaging the widest possible range of stakeholders, and creatively promoting existing and new resources and programs. The Critical Issues Program also provides a portal to decision-relevant, impartial geoscience information relevant to classroom discussions.

Program participants learned about three online videos by the **Center for Ocean Sciences Education Excellence** (COSEE) depicting dramatic changes in Alaska's marine ecosystems through interviews with scientists. The videos were produced by COSEE Alaska in cooperation with other geoscience organizations.

As promoted by Earth Science Week, the **Climate Literacy and Energy Awareness Network** (CLEAN) online portal stewards a collection of climate and energy science education resources and supports professionals committed to improving climate and energy literacy. Key components include the CLEAN collection of climate and energy science resources, CLEAN guidance and professional development webinars for teaching climate and energy science, and the CLEAN network of professionals committed to improving climate and energy literacy. For this year's Earth Science Week Toolkit, CLEAN provided a bookmark featuring a link to key resources.

The **Critical Zone Observatories** (CZO) provided an informational flyer featuring a "Humans and Soil Change" activity, for the Earth Science Week Toolkit in 2020. Earth Science Week participants also learned how to access resources on CZO's K–12 Education web page.

Earth Science Week participants were encouraged to celebrate **Earth Day** in April 2020 with educational activities, experiments, and investigations exploring the science behind how the world works. Because Earth Science Week offers education materials, information, and tools throughout the year, school audiences were urged to make use of tools highlighting the theme of "Earth Materials in Our Lives."

Program participants were notified of the sixth annual **Earth Educators' Rendezvous,** a virtual event, in July 2020. Workshops, oral and poster sessions, teaching demonstrations, panel discussions, and plenary talks were tailored to appeal to those working in Earth education, including college faculty, graduate students, K–12 teachers, informal educators, practitioners, administrators, and researchers.

ExxonMobil, a longtime Earth Science Week partner, continued its support of the program. During summer 2020, ExxonMobil Exploration and AGI partnered to hold their 12th annual Earth Science/STEM Teacher Leadership Academy. Traditionally held in Houston, the academy was retooled by AGI in 2020 to enable teachers to enjoy a high-quality professional development experience online. The academy provided K–8 teachers with Earth science content, hands-on activities to perform at home, resources and field experiences for them to use with their students and with their colleagues in professional development settings. ExxonMobil also supported Earth Science Week 2020 activities as a Global Sponsor.

For the Earth Science Week 2020 Toolkit, the **Gemological Institute of America** provided a GemKids poster exploring what gems are, how they are formed, how they are found, and how they are processed.

Through Earth Science Week, participants learned about educational resources and programs of the **Geological Society of America** (GSA), a longtime program partner. Featured education and outreach programs included the GeoTeacher program and Teacher GeoVenture trips. Program participants also learned about GSA's field awards for students, including the J. David Lowell Field Camp Scholarship and the GSA/ExxonMobil Bighorn Basin Field Award. GSA also organized International EarthCache Day at the start of Earth Science Week 2020 and contributed as an active partner in the Geologic Map Day initiative. Earth Science Week's 2020 activity calendar included GSA's "Mineral Matching" activity. Subscribers to the GSA Today magazine received copies of the Earth Science Week 2020 poster in the publication.

The **Geological Society of London** (GSL), an international Earth Science Week partner, offers a pair of online resources for learning about key geoscience topics. Electronic map-based resources are the focus of GSL's Plate Tectonics page. In addition, a site was launched to accompany GSL's Rock Cycle online module.

Program participants were directed to **Geology.com,** an Earth Science Week partner that provides a variety of geoscience materials as well as resources for teachers, including links to lesson plans from major Earth science organizations. Geology.com, in turn, covered Earth Science Week announcements, programs, and activities throughout the year.

For the Earth Science Week 2020 Toolkit, the **Geothermal Resources Council** provided an informational and colorful poster detailing the history, forms, and uses of geothermal energy (in both English and Spanish).

Through the Global Learning and Observations to Benefit the Environment (GLOBE) program, Earth Science Week participants learned how to take part in **GLOBE Observer,** an international network of professional scientists and citizen scientists collaborating to promote education about environment and climate.

To help teachers and students delve into the science behind current events, Earth Science Week continued to direct them to the **Incorporated Research Institutions for Seismology** (IRIS) website. IRIS provides educational resources including PowerPoint presentations, animations, and visualizations, as well as links to Spanish-language materials and USGS data that deal with current events such as earthquakes. For the 2020 educator kit, IRIS also provided a flyer detailing a number of free educational resources, including earthquake and seismology lessons, animations, videos, and more.

The **International Raw Materials Observatory** (Intraw) supported a wide range of Earth Science Week 2020 by becoming the program's first-ever Global Sponsor. Intraw helped promote awareness of the inaugural Minerals Day and the "Earth Materials Frontiers" Webinar Series.

Lyda Hill Philanthropies continued its partnership with AGI and Earth Science Week in 2020, supporting the launch of an initiative to share the inspiring stories of four leading women geoscientists recently named IF/THEN Ambassadors. To encourage the participation of young women in science, technology, engineering, and math (STEM) fields, Earth Science Week launched a new website featuring profiles of IF/THEN Ambassadors and educational activities linked to their work as geoscientists.

Earth Science Week participants tapped the educational offerings of program partner **Mineralogical Society of America** (MSA), especially in celebrating the launch of the first-ever Minerals Day on the Monday of Earth Science Week 2020. AGI and MSA jointly established the event to raise awareness of and appreciation for minerals. MSA developed materials, organized outreach, and collaborated with additional geoscience agencies, corporations, and nonprofits. MSA created a web page providing related educational resources and links. On the page, MSA provided two online minerals posters (one aimed at the general public, the other at K–12 students) available as printable PDFs. To help program participants prepare for the October celebration of Minerals Day, the September spread of Earth Science Week's 2020 activity calendar featured a "Change Over Time" learning activity courtesy of MSA. And AGI's "Earth Materials Frontiers" webinar series, which provided engaging content linked to learning about minerals, included webinars organized by MSA.

The **Minerals Education Coalition** (MEC) of the **Society for Mining, Metallurgy, and Exploration,** an AGI member society, supported Earth Science Week in 2020. MEC provided a "Sort It Out" postcard for the educator kit, as well as a 2019 calendar activity entitled "Sifting Stones."

The **MOSAiC (Multidisciplinary drifting Observatory for the Study of Arctic Climate)** expedition invited educators to connect students to one of the most extensive Arctic research expeditions ever conducted. From September 2019 through October 2020, more than 500 scientists from over 19 nations spent a year in the Arctic ice to collect data on Arctic climate. Through the MOSAiC Monday program, students tracked the expedition in real time on a map, graphed Arctic oceanographic data from the ship, watched video interviews with scientists and crewmembers, and engaged in short Arctic-related engagements linked to the Next Generation Science Standards.

Earth Science Week directed participants' attention to a joint effort by AGI and the **National Association of Geoscience Teachers** (NAGT) to strengthen implementation of the Next Generation Science Standards (NGSS) at the state level. Science educators have regularly participated in free webinars and joined discussions online since the 2015 NGSS Summit. Earth Science Week participants have been invited to take advantage of NAGT offerings including online lessons, NAGT's Outstanding Earth Science Teacher Awards, the Dorothy Stout Professional Development Grants, and the Journal of Geoscience Education.

NASA, a founding partner of Earth Science Week, provided materials in the Earth Science Week 2020 Toolkit as well as online. NASA included multiple resources in the educator kit, including an EO Kids "Shape of Farming: Water for Crops" flyer, an EO Kids "Water, Water Everywhere" flyer, and a "How Much Water Is on Earth" mini-poster. NASA also supported a "Factory Earth" poster and game provided by AmericaView for the 2020 educator kit, which allowed young people and others to explore topics including Earth materials, Landsat satellites, and Earth Observation Day. Earth Science Week's 2020 activity calendar also featured a "Carbon Travels" classroom activity from NASA. Throughout the year, Earth Science Week promoted awareness of NASA's online offerings, such as the Diversity & Inclusion Leadership Video Series, the For Educators portal, EO Kids, NASA Educator Toolkit, National Parks from Space, Earth Wheel, NASA Earth Observatory, Mapping Our World Interactive, NASA STEM Engagement, and NASA Wavelength. NASA also continued to serve as an active partner in Geologic Map Day.

Justin Xu's winning entry for the ESW 2020 Visual Arts Contest

The **National Earth Science Teaching Association** (NESTA), a longtime Earth Science Week partner, continued its vital role in helping AGI promote excellence in geoscience education. In connection with the National Science Teaching Association Annual Conference, the NESTA Reception included a ceremony during which a teacher was given the Edward C. Roy Jr. Award for Excellence in K–8 Earth Science Teaching. NESTA members also received copies of the Earth Science Week 2020 poster in their association newsletter.

Earth Science Week raised awareness of **National Environmental Education Week** (EE Week), the nation's largest environmental education event. Focusing largely on STEM topics, EE Week connected educators with resources to promote K–12 students' understanding of the environment.

Educators were invited to apply for the Grosvenor Teacher Fellowship program organized by the **National Geographic Society** with Lindblad Expeditions. This program recognizes pre-K–12 classroom teachers and informal educators who show dedication to geographic education.

Earth Science Week promoted the **National Groundwater Association**'s (NGWA) Groundwater Awareness Week in March 2020. The AGI member society offers Groundwater Adventures, a website providing educational activities for young people.

Earth Science Week's 2020 activity calendar also featured a "Engineering Biodegradable Drifters" learning activity from the **National Oceanic and Atmospheric Administration** (NOAA). In addition, Earth Science Week 2020 directed participants to NOAA's online multimedia education resources, including lesson plans, real-world data, instructional games, videos, and more.

A longtime Earth Science Week partner, the **National Park Service** (NPS) continued for the 11th year a major component to its involvement in Earth Science Week: National Fossil Day, established as a celebration to take place annually on the Wednesday of Earth Science Week, once again reached millions of people. Earth Science Week promoted awareness of NPS's interactive Web Ranger program, which helps people of all ages learn about the national parks. The NPS National Fossil Day art contest engaged students and others. Earth Science Week participants learned about unique online resource launched by the National Park Service in partnership with AGI, "Virtual Field Trip: Air Quality at Shenandoah National Park," which incorporates interactive features allowing visitors to virtually explore the park, enjoying beautiful park vistas while learning about scientific contributions that the park makes to our understanding of air quality. Program participants also learned about the NPS National Natural Landmarks program, which recognizes and encourages the conservation of sites that contain outstanding biological and geological resources. NPS videos on climate change were made available to program participants. A postcard promoting National Fossil Day and paleontology awareness was included in the Earth Science Week Toolkit. Earth Science Week's 2020 activity calendar also featured an NPS classroom activity titled "Ring of Fire." NPS also was an ongoing partner in Geologic Map Day activities.

For the Earth Science Week 2020 Toolkit, the **National Science Foundation** provided worksheets on the water cycle and the science of rocks.

Earth Science Week partnered with the **National Science Teaching Association** (NSTA) again in 2020, reaching science educators nationwide. Program participants learned about "Freebies for Science Teachers" on the NSTA website. Also, AGI participated once again at the NSTA National Conference, sharing Earth Science Week and other education material for science teachers.

Earth Science Week participants learned about K–12 soil resources offered online by the **Natural Resource Conservation Service** (NRCS). Resources for the elementary level include frequently asked questions even soil songs. Middle and high school level resources include soil facts, health and quality, and state-specific soil information. Lesson plans and other resources are also accompanied by links to other websites.

AGI and its publishing partner **Nautilus,** which hosts AGI's EARTH online news channel, produced print booklets for distribution along with many Earth Science Week 2020 Toolkits. The Nautilus booklets feature profiles of four scientists featured on AGI's new Geoscience Women in STEM website. Subscribers to the print edition of Nautilus saw an Earth Science Week 2020 one-page ad in the magazine.

Newmont Corporation supported Earth Science Week 2020 as a Global Sponsor and helped promote awareness of various program activities via social media.

As the organizer of Earth Science Week, AGI collaborating with the **NGSS-ESS Working Group** to promote a number of free webinars available for enrichment among geoscience educators throughout the year. Webinars such as one titled "Beyond Earthquake Locations: Modern Seismology in the NGSS Classroom" provided teachers with support in instruction dealing with the Next Generation Science Standards (NGSS) in Earth System Science (ESS).

For the Earth Science Week 2020 Toolkit, the **Nutrients for Life Foundation** provided its "Are You in the H_2Know about H_2O?" flyer featuring a puzzle, a quiz, and a learning activity linked to NGSS science standards.

Gearing up for National Fossil Day, Earth Science Week directed program partners' attention to the **Paleontological Research Institution** (PRI), an AGI member society providing education materials and opportunities for science teachers and students at all grade levels. The online Teacher Friendly Guide, for example, gives brief geologic histories of every region of the United States.

For the Earth Science Week 2020 Toolkit, the **Paleontological Society** provided a flyer connecting participants with online resources including Fossil Fact Cards, a card-sorting activity linked to NGSS science education standards.

Longtime program partner **Partners in Resource Education** (PRE) provided activities focusing on the geoscience of conservation. The consortium of seven federal agencies educates thousands of young people, introduces them to natural resource careers, and cultivates the next generation of land and water stewards. In 2020, PRE collaborated to promote awareness of Earth Science Week, and vice versa.

Earth Science Week promoted the educational offerings of the **Seismological Society of America,** which links online visitors to resources including geoscience activities related to seismic science and earthquakes. A website features seismic eruption models, wave animations, plate tectonics simulations, information on tsunamis, and much more.

For teachers aiming to "shake up" education, Earth Science Week shone a spotlight on the **Seismological Society of America** (SSA). SSA's website provided seismic eruption models, wave animations, plate tectonics simulations, information on tsunamis, and more. SSA also offered publications, information on seismology careers, a distinguished lecturer series, and an electronic encyclopedia of earthquakes.

Earth Science Week alerted participants to the fact that **SEPM – The Society for Sedimentary Geology** offered funding for students studying sedimentary geoscience or related areas to attend the first International Sedimentary Geoscience Congress in April 2020.

Earth Science Week participants were encouraged to take advantage of offerings of the **Society of Exploration Geophysicists** (SEG), which provides programs for educators and students. For example, the distinguished lecturer series and honorary lecturer series both enabled students to meet professional geophysicists, learn about groundbreaking research in the field of seismic research, and obtain valuable career information. SEG's "What Do Geophysicists Do?" promoted awareness of ways that geophysicists make a difference with innovations addressing energy, water, and climate. Highlighting insights inspired by SEG's Geoscientists Without Borders programs, the Earth Science Week 2020 activity calendar featured a "Humanitarian Geoscience" classroom activity from SEG. Subscribers to SEG's The Leading Edge viewed an Earth Science Week 2020 ad in the magazine.

Advanced by the **Society of Petroleum Engineers** (SPE), the Energy4Me program offers teachers a collection of tools for teaching about oil, gas, and other energy sources, including classroom activities, experiments, and presentations, as well as teacher workshops and energy education materials for the classroom. Earth Science Week's 2020 activity calendar included a "Core Sampling" classroom activity from Enegy4Me.

The **Soil Science Society of America** (SSSA), a longtime program partner, provides lessons, activities, fun facts, sites of interest, and soil definitions for the novice soil scientist online. These resources were promoted by the October event. For the Earth Science Week 2020 Toolkit, SSSA provided a flyer with information and links

A finalist entry for the 2020 ESW Photography Contest submitted by Jessica Malkin

to educational resources on soil science. Earth Science Week's 2020 activity calendar also featured a "Nature's Water Filter" classroom activity courtesy of SSSA.

SWITCH Energy Alliance provided a sticky-note pad promoting its "Switch On" program for the Earth Science Week 2020 Toolkit. Program participants also learned about "Switch On," a new film featuring Dr. Scott Tinker available to stream online.

For the Earth Science Week 2020 Toolkit, **UNAVCO** provided an English-language sticker and a Spanish-language poster about "measuring Earth and atmosphere from Alaska to Aruba."

The **U.S. Bureau of Land Management** (BLM), a continuing Earth Science Week partner, provided a flyer including a dinosaur activity sheet for the 2020 educator kit. BLM also was the subject of Earth Science Week promotions, including its Classroom Investigation Series online.

The **U.S. Department of Energy** (DOE) invited educators to explore DOE's websites for the National Renewable Energy Laboratory. Earth Science Week participants were made aware that AGI's Center for Geoscience & Society produced education materials, including videos in English and Spanish, education guides, a "quick start" guide to energy literacy, lesson connections, and guidance on aligning energy literacy lessons with the Next Generation Science Standards. Essential Principles and Fundamental Concepts for Energy Education resources were made available on the DOE website.

Earth Science Week also promoted awareness of the **U.S. Environmental Protection Agency**'s collection of free resources to enhance middle school students' understanding of climate change impacts on the United States' wildlife and ecosystems. The online toolkit includes case studies, activities, and videos based on climate science, environmental education, and stewardship information.

Overlapping Earth Science Week 2020, National Wildlife Refuge Week was held October 11–17. The event, celebrating the richness of the 550 units that make up America's National Wildlife Refuge System, was sponsored once again by the **U.S. Fish and Wildlife Service** (FWS). Earth Science Week participants were encouraged to safely explore geoscience at a wildlife refuge.

For the Earth Science Week 2020 Toolkit, the U.S. Forest Service provided a "Stories in Stone" postcard presenting information on the geology of the National Forest System and its Minerals and Geology Management Program, as well as links for more.

Earth Science Week participants learned about online education resources offered by the **U.S. Geological Survey** (USGS), a longtime Earth Science Week partner and supporter, as well as the thousands of free images and over 69,000 searchable publications such as maps, books, and charts provided online by the agency. USGS distributed flyers detailing the raw materials in cellphones and U.S. Navy SEAL gear as part of the Earth Science Week Toolkit. USGS also supported a "Factory Earth" poster and game provided by AmericaView for the educator kit, enabling participants to explore Earth materials, Landsat satellites, and Earth Observation Day. Earth Science Week's 2020 activity calendar included a "Minerals Under Your Roof" activity courtesy of USGS. Also, USGS continued its leadership role as a founding partner of Geologic Map Day, providing support as well as its National Geologic Map Database's MapView, which offers a mosaic view of published geologic maps.

Earth Science Week participants were invited to explore the **U.S. Global Change Research Program**'s "Climate Change, Wildlife, and Wildlands Toolkit for Formal and Informal Educators." The U.S. Environmental Protection Agency (in partnership with National Park Service, U.S. Fish and Wildlife Service, NOAA, NASA, U.S. Forest Service, and Bureau of Land Management) developed the kit, which is designed for teachers and informal educators in settings such as parks, refuges, forest lands, nature centers, zoos, aquariums, and science centers.

Earth Science Week 2020 helped participants estimate their water-usage habits with the GRACE Communications Foundation's **Water Footprint Calculator.** This online tool illustrates how people's actions impact water use, asking a series of questions about daily activities calculating the number of gallons used after each question. The educator kit also featured a postcard promoting the program.

Program participants learned about the **William T. Pecora Award,** presented annually to individuals or groups that have made outstanding contributions toward understanding the Earth by means of remote sensing. The award is sponsored by the U.S. Department of the Interior and NASA.

Earth Science Week continued promoting awareness of **Windows on Earth,** an online educational project that features photographs taken by astronauts on the International Space Station. The site is operated by TERC, an educational non-profit, in collaboration with the Association of Space Explorers (the professional association of flown astronauts and cosmonauts), the Virtual High School, and CASIS (Center for Advancement of Science in Space). The images help show Earth from a global perspective.

Earth Science Week Toolkits

AGI assembled some **10,000 Earth Science Week Toolkits,** the majority of which were distributed to teachers and geoscientists before the end of 2020. Thirteen AGI member societies requested complimentary Earth Science Week Toolkits for distribution, and 27 state geological surveys requested complimentary kits for distribution.

As in past years, thousands of kits also were **distributed through program partners** including USGS, NASA, the National Park Service, and AAPG student chapters. Toolkits were shipped to program participants in 28 nations around the world. The 2020 toolkit featured AGI's traditional Earth Science Week poster, education and outreach flyers, and school-year calendar showcasing geoscience classroom investigations and important dates of Earth science events.

Continuing recent years' trend, the 2020–21 school-year calendar's classroom investigations featured notations explaining to educators how each activity aligns with expectations outlined in the **Next Generation Science Standards.** Additionally, program partners' contributions, many of which also included activities aligned with the standards, made the Earth Science Week 2020 Toolkit one of the richest ever.

The **Online Toolkit** included downloadable resources available from past Earth Science Week celebrations. Users can browse resources by theme/year, type of resource, and Next Generation Science Standards (NGSS) topics. The Online Toolkit houses resources dating back to 2014 and is a feasible option to organizations that want to lower their paper use, as well as users who are limited by shipping and printing costs.

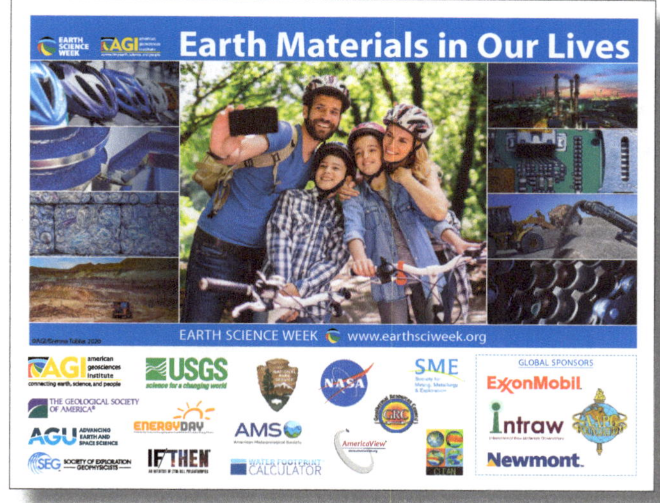

2020 ESW Toolkit folder from AGI

Web Resources

According to Google Analytics, the **Earth Science Week website** was accessed by users in **212 nations, territories, and regions** worldwide in 2020. The program website (www.earthsciweek.org) delivers essential resources for educators throughout the year. As in past years, the Earth Science Week website was updated regularly to reflect the new theme, contests, proclamations, events, initiatives, and classroom activities for 2020. The entire site received more than 494,000 page views in 2020, up from the previous year. Within the site, all searches made in 2020 related to specific pages totaled 337,757 for Classroom Activities, 20,186 for Contests, 7,891 for Big Ideas Activities, and 1,988 for Focus Days.

The most significant addition to Earth Science Week's online offerings in 2020 may have been the launch of the **Geoscience Women in STEM website,** providing Earth science teaching and learning resources inspired by the geoscience-related work of leading women scientists and engineers, with support from Lyda Hill Philanthropies. AGI produced the site to strengthen geoscience education through the stories of women in geoscience, including some recently selected as AAAS IF/THEN Ambassadors by IF/THEN®, an initiative created by Lyda Hill Philanthropies to encourage and elevate the participation of girls and women in science, technology, engineering, and math (STEM). The site offers curriculum connections that focus on the Next Generation Science Standards in Earth and Space Science (NGSS-ESS) and illuminate ways that STEM topics can be explored across traditional disciplinary boundaries. In 2020 the site furthered the Earth Science Week 2019 theme of "Geoscience Is for Everyone," which promoted both the inclusive potential and the importance of the geosciences in the lives of all people. AGI unveiled the completed website with a free NGSS-ESS Working Group webinar, "Promoting Diversity in the Geosciences: Meet the Geoscience Women in STEM," introducing teachers to curriculum modules developed around the inspirational stories of trailblazing women in STEM fields.

In collaboration with the Mineralogical Society of America, the International Raw Materials Observatory, and additional partners, AGI hosted the **"Earth Materials Frontiers" Webinar Series,** available during Earth Science Week 2020 and beyond. This series of nine webinars covered thought-provoking, timely topics relating to the theme of "Earth Materials in Our Lives," including gemology, crystallography, the mineralogy of Mars, space exploration for raw materials, robotics in mining, conflict minerals, and critical mineral commodities. Selected on-demand webinars had live question-and-answer periods with presenters. Aimed at the general public and education community, webinars were available in 62 languages with multilingual captioning. The webinars, originally broadcast live October 12–16, 2020, remain available online.

Working with a coalition of organizations, AGI also encouraged Earth Science Week participants to take part in the **"America's Geoheritage II: Identifying, Developing, and Preserving America's Natural Legacy" Distinguished Speaker Webinar Series.** The series of eight free webinars presented a range of topics related to geoheritage that could be connected to curriculum and instruction in several subject areas. Continuing education credit was available for educators who participated in the series. The webinar series was organized by the Board on International Scientific Organizations, U.S. National Committee for Geological Sciences, National Academies of Sciences, Engineering, and Medicine. Supported by the National Science Foundation, the series was sponsored by the American Association of State

Geologists, Geological Society of America, National Association of Geoscience Teachers, National Earth Science Teachers Association, National Park Service, and U.S. Geological Survey, and AGI.

Earth Science Week participants were invited to download or print the new **Critical Needs in Geoscience Mini-Poster** available digitally online in 2020. AGI and its federation of geoscience societies collaborated to provide an overview of critical issues and policy recommendations for the next presidential administration, federal agencies, and the U.S. Congress. AGI's mini-poster summarizes the key points of the full document, "Geosciences Supporting a Thriving Society in a Changing World," which informs policymakers about ways that the geoscience knowledge, experience, and ingenuity can address society's most pressing issues.

Promoting high-quality learning activities that stimulate experiential learning and mobilize conceptual thinking in the geosciences, Earth Science Week hosted its **Diversity, Equity, and Inclusion Strategies** page for educators online. The page shows how inclusive activities can be geared to serve the needs of all learners — regardless of age, background, or identity — allowing them to participate fully in the learning process. A selection of strategies designed to support inclusive activities is organized under headings given in the Next Generation Science Standards. Each strategy is accompanied by an example of a related geoscience-focused learning experience.

Program participants hosting events during Earth Science Week 2020 were invited to let people know about it at **Events in Your Area.** This web page provided information on events taking place through program partners in each state, such as exhibits, tours, lectures, and open houses. The **Earth Science Week Event Registry** enabled participants to promote their events more effectively than ever. All registered events were listed on Earth Science Week's **Events in Your Area** site.

In addition, participating groups could be listed in **Earth Science Organizations,** an online map that offers clickable links to Earth Science Week events taking place at parks, museums, science and technology centers, university geology departments, local geological societies, and other nearby locations.

Promoted through various online channels, AGI's **Earth Science Week promotional video** trumpeted the importance of the geosciences and the celebration's role in promoting public awareness. This brief, exciting, eye-popping video answers key questions: Why is Earth science a big deal? How does Earth Science Week help promote understanding? And what can viewers do to get involved?

While exploring the Earth Science Week theme of "Earth Materials in Our Lives," science teachers and students were invited to consider the ways that people showcase and access information on Earth systems in a variety of forums. The **Our Shared Geoheritage** and **Visualizing Earth Systems** pages continue to be popular resources on the Earth Science Week website. Our Geological Heritage features educational material on this heritage and links users to recommended resources, including downloadable reports, articles, blogs, geoheritage locations, and learning activities. The page also features geoheritage-related classroom activities and links to information on geoheritage in every state. Visualizing Earth Systems links users to dozens of recommended visualizations dealing with energy, climate, minerals, water, hazards, and other topics. In addition, the page links users to overviews of these topics provided by AGI's Critical Issues Program.

Once again AGI offered four quarterly **Earth Science Week Webcasts** in 2020, expanding the program's use of online formats and media for public outreach. The free webcasts provided lively overviews of Focus Days (spring), Contests (summer), the Toolkit (autumn), and the Roy Award (winter). Each roughly five-minute tutorial includes a wealth of online links, which viewers can click during the narrated presentation to review available resources.

Program participants were encouraged to visit the continually updated Earth Science Week **Classroom Activities** page for more than 200 free learning activities, most contributed by leading geoscience agencies and groups. To find an activity corresponding to a lesson, teachers can search by Earth science topic, grade level, and science education standard.

AGI provided a set of free online videos and other electronic resources to help students, educators, and others explore the "big ideas" of Earth science during Earth Science Week 2020 and throughout the year. **Big Ideas Videos** bring to life the nine core geoscience concepts that everyone should know. The Earth Science Literacy Initiative, funded by the National Science Foundation, codified these principles. The videos are available on YouTube and TeacherTube. The Earth Science Week website also provides dozens of classroom activities linked to the "big ideas."

Finally, Earth Science Week makes ample use of online social networking to reach new audiences, especially young people. The program's presence on **Facebook,** the Internet's most popular networking site, includes an Earth Science Week Fan Page. In addition, web surfers are invited to receive geoscience news, resources, and opportunities by following Earth Science Week on **Twitter.** Tweets are sent frequently, whenever there is valuable news or information to share. The number of people learning about Earth Science Week through social media remained impressive in 2020, with the program attracting more than 6,400 Facebook follows and over 206,000 Twitter impressions.

Newsletter

The monthly **Earth Science Week Update** newsletter reached some 5,000 teacher, student, and geoscientist subscribers in the past year. The electronic newsletter kept planners and participants up to date on Earth Science Week planning at the national level, encouraged participation in local areas, and provided news on geoscience topics of interest to participants. Besides highlighting worthwhile resources, these monthly e-mail updates reinforce the belief that geoscience education is a priority throughout the year, not only for one week each October.

Contests

AGI held contests in connection with Earth Science Week for the 20th consecutive year. Contests were designed to encourage K–12 students, teachers, and the general public to become involved in the celebration by exploring artistic and academic applications of Earth science. Earth Science Week continued expanded eligibility for its photo contest to allow international members of **AGI Member Societies** and **AGI International Affiliates** to participate.

Four contests continued to provide ways for many people to participate in Earth Science Week. Hundreds of submissions were received. Each first-place winner received $300 and an AGI publication. Entries submitted by winners and finalists were posted online.

Justin Xu of Sugar Hill, Georgia, won first place in the visual arts contest, **"Earth Materials and Me."** Finalists were Teagin Costanzo of Mauldin, South Carolina;

Elizabeth Xu, for the ESW 2020 Visual Arts Contest

Everett Lee of Fargo, North Dakota; Elizabeth Xu of Sugar Hill, Georgia; and Nathan Xu of Clyde Hill, Washington. Students in grades K–5 made two-dimensional artworks illustrating how Earth materials play a role in their lives.

Alex Xu of Clyde Hill, Washington, won first place in the photo contest, **"Earth Materials in My Community."** Finalists were Evan Costa of Chepachet, Rhode Island; Ella Giguere of San Carlos, California; Tori Judy of Belmont, California; and Jessica Malkin of Grand Rapids, Michigan. Submissions illustrated the theme "Earth Materials in My Community."

Akhshith Rengaraju of Aurora, Illinois, won first place in the essay contest, **"How We Process Earth Materials."** Finalists were Korina Cortezano of Virginia Beach,

Everett Lee, for the ESW 2020 Visual Arts Contest

Virginia; Archelaus Paxon of El Paso, Texas; Rachel Xu of Gainesville, Florida; and Clara Zabik of Chagrin Falls, Ohio. Students in grades 6–9 wrote essays of up to 300 words exploring ways people can develop practices and policies that allow them to derive practical value from raw materials while maintaining community values.

Isabella Van Deman and Faith Qin (team) of Virginia Beach, Virginia won first place in the video contest, **"Earth Materials Around the World."** Finalists were Achyut Balaji of Hillsboro, Oregon; Shreya Dhanala of Folsom, California; Jeremiah Johnson-Reynolds of Blythewood, South Carolina; Sri Utami of Pamukkale, Denizli Province, Turkey. Individuals and teams created brief, original videos that show how people of various backgrounds around the world make the most of Earth materials.

Nathan Xu, for the ESW 2020 Visual Arts Contest

Evan Costa, for the 2020 ESW Photography Contest

Tori Judy, for the 2020 ESW Photography Contest

Our Next Step
by Akhshith Rengaraju, for the 2020 ESW
Essay Contest

As intelligent civilizations, we've advanced from the Stone Age to the Modern Age by utilizing natural resources from the Earth. But we don't always ponder about how they're processed. Our world is shaped by the dangerous effects this can cause, such as global warming and the loss of biodiversity.

We, the young generation of the future have the responsibility and potential to change our world for the better. Schools should enforce a policy to have a mandatory class named "Earth Solutions", where students are educated about "Reuse, Reduce, and Refuse". Students should also be made aware of all unnecessary products which aren't biodegradable and develop a practice of completely avoiding one-use items. These can include plastics, decorative items for celebrations, styrofoam products, and ceramics. Additionally, we should be taught about our "Needs and Wants" considering the environment.

*Read the rest of this essay on the **ESW website**.*

Earth Science Teaching Award

For the 13th consecutive year, AGI and the AGI Foundation offered the **Edward C. Roy Jr. Award for Excellence in K–8 Earth Science Teaching.** The 2020 award went to Sherry Claflin, an eighth-grade Earth science teacher at White Cloud Junior High School in White Cloud, Michigan. In addition to teaching Earth science in her current position, Claflin has served as an editor and contributing writer for Michigan Earth Scientist, an adjunct geology instructor at Muskegon Community College, a teacher at Annis Water Resources Institute, and an education and outreach consultant for the Newaygo Conservation District's Stephen F. Wessling Observatory and Kropscott Farm Environmental Center.

Claflin received a $2,500 prize and an additional grant of $1,000 to enable her to undertake professional development activities of her choosing. Claflin was presented with the award during a virtual reception hosted by the National Earth Science Teachers Association at the online conference of the National Science Teaching Association.

The award recognizes one classroom teacher from kindergarten to eighth grade for leadership and innovation in Earth science education. This award is named in honor of Dr. Edward C. Roy Jr., a past president of AGI and strong supporter of Earth science education. In addition to U.S. teachers, instructors throughout the United Kingdom were invited to compete for the prize. U.K. teachers were provided with detailed guidance on entering the competition by AGI and **The Geological Society of London**, a member society and Earth Science Week partner.

Focus Days

Earth Science Week 2020 kicked off on Sunday, October 11, with the 13th annual **International EarthCache Day**. "EarthCaching" is a variation of a recreational activity known as geocaching, in which a geocache organizer posts latitude and longitude coordinates on the Internet to advertise a cache that geocachers locate using GPS devices. When people visit an EarthCache, they learn something special about Earth science, the geology of the location, or how the Earth's resources and environment are managed there. EarthCaching has been developed by the Geological Society of America, a major Earth Science Week program partner.

On Monday, October 12, educators, young people, and mineral enthusiasts of all ages were encouraged to take part in the first-ever **Minerals Day.** AGI and the Mineralogical Society of America (MSA) launched Minerals Day to raise awareness of and appreciation for minerals among the general public as well as students and teachers of all ages and at all levels. Dovetailing with the Earth Science Week 2020 theme of "Earth Materials in Our Lives," Minerals Day introduced participants to a host of educational resources and activities focusing on the role of raw materials in the lives of individuals and in society. AGI and MSA both launched Minerals Day web pages to spur activity and provide resources in an educational climate shaped by the coronavirus pandemic. The partners developed materials, organized outreach, and collaborated with additional geoscience agencies, corporations, and nonprofits such as museums, libraries, and rock and mineral clubs to promote the event. For example, organizations such as the Minerals Education Coalition and the Museum of Natural Sciences North Carolina promoted Minerals Day online. To help program participants prepare for the October celebration of Minerals Day, the September central spread of Earth Science Week's 2020 activity calendar featured a "Change Over Time" learning activity courtesy of MSA. AGI's "Earth Materials Frontiers" webinar series provided engaging content linked to learning about minerals, including webinars organized by MSA, during the weeklong celebration. And AGI and MSA each used social media platforms to promoting Minerals Day during the weeks leading up to the event.

On the Tuesday of Earth Science Week 2020, participants were invited to take part in **Earth Observation Day.** Previously celebrated at other times of the year, this October 13 event aimed to engage students and teachers in remote sensing as an exciting and powerful educational tool. The event was a STEM educational outreach event of AmericaView and its partners. AmericaView is a nationwide partnership of remote sensing scientists who support the use of Landsat and other public domain remotely sensed satellite data through applied remote sensing research, K–12 and higher STEM education, workforce development, and technology transfer. Participants made use of lessons and activities by AmericaView and other organizations, as well as additional Earth Observation Day resources, online.

One of the highlights of recent years' Earth Science Week celebrations has been **"No Child Left Inside" Day,** an event that in its inaugural year (2008) engaged some 500 students in outdoor learning activities and received coverage by news media from NBC to NPR. In 2020, students and educators nationwide were encouraged to engage in safe, educational activities outdoors on the Tuesday of Earth Science Week, October 13. AGI's online NCLI Day Guide provided everything needed to plan a local NCLI Day event. The free guide provides 17 outdoor activities, as well as detailed recommendations for creating partnerships, planning logistics, reaching out to the local media, and following up in instruction.

Earth Science featured the return of a popular event, **National Fossil Day**. In partnership with the National Park Service (NPS), AGI helped conduct the 11th annual event, officially on Wednesday, October 14, including activities and resources designed to celebrate the scientific and educational value of fossils, paleontology, and the importance of preserving fossils for future generations. NPS offered a website full of educational resources and information designed specifically for students and teachers. On the site's NPS Fossil Park Highlights page, visitors could find lesson plans developed to reflect state standards, fossil trading cards, videos about pygmy mammoths, special brochures, a virtual museum exhibit on dinosaurs, and more. NPS also held a National Fossil Day Art Contest that engaged program participants.

Program participants were invited to join the Earth Science Week team in encouraging everyone — including women, minorities, and people with a range of abilities — to explore geoscience careers on **Geoscience for Everyone Day,** Thursday, October 15. The aim was to open a young person's eyes to the world of Earth science. Doing so, participants supported the efforts of AGI member societies such as the Association for Women Geoscientists and the National Association of Black Geoscientists in raising awareness of the remarkable opportunities available to all young people in the Earth sciences. The program website directed participants to "Visiting Geoscientists: An Outreach Guide for Geoscience Professionals," a handbook co-produced by AGI and the American Association of Petroleum Geologists' Youth Education Activities Committee.

The ninth annual **Geologic Map Day** held on Friday, October 16, 2019, promoted awareness of the study, uses, and importance of geologic mapping for education, science, business, and a variety of public policy concerns. The final event for the school week of Earth Science Week 2020 was hosted by the U.S. Geological Survey and the Association of American State Geologists in partnership with AGI, along with additional partners including

Teagin Costanzo, for the ESW 2020 Visual Arts Contest

the National Park Service, the Geological Society of America, and NASA. Students, teachers, and the wider public tapped into the various educational activities, print materials, online resources, and public outreach opportunities for active participation. The Earth Science Week 2020 Toolkit contained a Geologic Map Day poster that provided geologic maps, plus step-by-step instructions for a related classroom activity dealing with Earth materials. Additional resources for learning about geologic maps were featured on the Geologic Map Day web page of the Earth Science Week site.

Earth Science Week 2020 reached its climax with **International Archaeology Day** on Saturday, October 17. The event was a celebration of archaeology and the thrill of discovery. Every October, archaeological programs and activities for people of all ages and interests are presented by the Archaeological Institute of America and archaeological organizations across the United States, Canada, and elsewhere. Activities provided the chance for participants to indulge their inner "Indiana Jones."

AGI Promotions

Earth Science Week promoted awareness of numerous AGI programs and resources of interest to Earth science educators, students, and enthusiasts, including AGI's Center for Geoscience & Society, the AGI Geoscience Workforce program, AGI Scholarly Information (including GeoRef), AGI's Teacher Leadership Academy, Geoscience Currents, the William L. Fisher Congressional Geoscience Fellowship, AGI Summer Internships, AGI's NGSS Education Webinars, the Pulse of Earth Science website, the Visiting Geoscientists guide, AGI's Critical Issues Program, AGI's Career Compass infographics, Geoscience in Your State Factsheets, the Earth Science Organizations website, the Faces of Earth four-part film series, the EARTH Channel on Nautilus magazine online, the award-winning Why Earth Science video, and the Why Earth Science brochure.

To assist geoscience students, educators, and other professionals at a time when many were working remotely or in new ways during the pandemic, AGI announced the availability of several electronic resources for free or at reduced prices, including AGI's Education GeoSource, Glossary of Geology, Geoscience Handbook, professional development modules, and more. AGI alerted educators to the availability of dozens of modules in the free-to-take Geoscience Online Learning Initiative (GOLI) platform. To support geoscience faculty who are moving to an online teaching format, AGI's publishing partner, Pearson, provided free e-text of the AGI/NAGT Lab Manual in Physical Geology to all adopters of that manual. These resources complimented the many offerings already available through the Earth Science Week website.

State Proclamations

Seven states have demonstrated outstanding science-literacy leadership by issuing **"perpetual proclamations"** of Earth Science Week, ensuring recognition every year: Alaska, Delaware, Illinois, Nevada, North Dakota, Oklahoma, and South Dakota.

Governors also issued single-year proclamations in six additional states — Alabama, Missouri, Nevada, Oregon, Pennsylvania, and Virginia — bringing the total number of states with proclamations of recognizing Earth Science Week 2020 to 13.

Publicity and Media Coverage

AGI enlisted the support of a wide range of media in promoting awareness of Earth Science Week, resulting in exceptional reach for promotional activities in 2020 and helping to lay a foundation for more coverage in years to come. Because of the large number of news clips citing Earth Science Week activities and resources, the print edition of this report no longer includes such clips. To view the many news items dealing with Earth Science Week, please visit online at **www.earthsciweek. org/highlights.**

Earth Science Week 2020 news, events, programs, and resources were covered by **international news organizations** including Atlas Obscura, AU Scope (Australia), b93.fm (Canada), Belgian Earth Observation (Belgium), Earth Science Partnership (Wales), Emirates News Agency (United Arab Emirates), European Geosciences Union (EGU), EuroWeekly (Spain), Facebook, Instagram, MENAFN (United Arab Emirates), Nature World News, The RiotACT (Australia), Samakal (Bangladesh), Taylor & Francis Group (England), and The World News Monitor (United Arab Emirates).

Additionally, the event was covered by **national news organizations** such as the Archaeological Institute of America, Critical Zone Observatories, Dates.Cloud, DeviantArt, EventBrite, Frost Science, Geocaching.com, Izzit.org, mBlip, National Day Calendar, National Park Service, News Track Live, Odessa America Online, The Pew Charitable Trusts, PICK Education, Planeta.com, The New York Times Puzzle Page, Reddit, and The River Houses.

Throughout the United States, coverage of Earth Science Week programs and activities was provided by **regional/ local news organizations** such as 1808 Delaware (Delaware), The Advertiser Tribune (Ohio), Alabama Museum of Natural History (Alabama), AllEvents.In Fruita (Colorado), AllEvents.In Gallatin (Tennessee), AllEvents.In Glen Mill (Pennsylvania), The Argus Observer (Oregon), Arizona State University (Arizona), Asheville Museum of Science (AMOS) (North Carolina), Basin Now (Utah), Bighorn Basin Paleontological Institute (Massachusetts), Blue Mountain Eagle (Oregon), Boston Parents Paper (Massachusetts), The Bryan News (Ohio), California Department of Conservation (California), Camp Verde Bugle (Arizona), Cañon City Daily Record (Colorado), Canton Public Library (Michigan), Casa Grande Valley Newspapers (Arizona), CASE News (Florida), Chicago Public Library, Chiefland Citizen (Florida), City of Phoenix (Arizona), Clark-Floyd Counties Convention-Tourism Bureau (Indiana), The Clermont Sun (Ohio), Cotsen Institute of Archaeology (UCLA) (California), Daily Journal Online (Missouri), Delaware Geological Survey (Delaware), Discovery Park of America (Tennessee), Earth Science Club of Northern Illinois (ESCONI) (Illinois), Elkhorn Media Group (Oregon), Explore Washington CT (Connecticut), Exploring by the Seat of Your Pants (Wyoming), Fort Hays State University (Kansas), Garden of the Gods Visitor & Nature Center (Colorado), The Gazette-Democrat (Illinois), Greater Boston Convention & Visitors Bureau (Massachusetts), Hays Convention & Visitors Bureau (Kansas), Houston Geological Society (Texas), HulaFrog (Pennsylvania), Idaho Geological Survey (Idaho), Idaho State Journal (Idaho),

Independence Bulletin Journal (Iowa), IowaView (Iowa), Kids Out and About (New York), KU Biodiversity Institute and Natural History Museum (Kansas), Lake Superior Magazine (Michigan), Las Cruces Bulletin (New Mexico), Lost City Museum (Nevada), Macaroni Kid, Marion County News (Tennessee), Marion Star (Ohio), Meetup (Colorado), Missouri Department of Natural Resources (Missouri), Missouri State (Missouri), Mommy Poppins (Connecticut), Murfreesboro Voice (Tennessee), Museum of Indian Arts & Culture (New Mexico), Museum of the Rockies (Montana), Museums of Western Colorado (Colorado), Naperville Park District (Illinois), Near North Now (Michigan), Nevada Today (Nevada), New Jersey Geological and Water Survey (New Jersey), New Mexico Bureau of Geology (New Mexico), New Mexico Bureau of Geology & Mineral Resources (New Mexico), Newton STEM (Massachusetts), Office for the Arts (Harvard University) (Massachusetts), Ohio History Connection (Ohio), Oklahoma Historical Society (Oklahoma), Orton Geological Museum (Ohio), Patch (Massachusetts), Penn Museum (Pennsylvania), Penn State News (Pennsylvania), Pennsylvania Department of Conservation and Natural Resources (Pennsylvania), Phelps County Focus (Missouri), Philly Fun Guide (Pennsylvania), Pinal Geology & Mineral Museum (Arizona), The Registered Citizen (Connecticut), Rice Museum of Rocks & Minerals (Oregon), RiverBender.com (Illinois), Rock and Mineral Shows (Idaho), SEMO Events (Missouri), SocialMiami.com (Florida), Soco Today (Colorado), The Soul of Miami (Florida), SPL Children's Department, Spot On Florida (Florida), StepOutside (Indiana), Sun Englewood (Florida), The Sun Newspapers (New Jersey), Tahlequah Daily Press (Oklahoma), Tennessee Department of Environment and Conservation (TDEC) (Tennessee), Todayheadline (Utah), The Tribune (Colorado), Tulane University (Louisiana), Union County Library System (Pennsylvania), University of Kentucky News (Kentucky), University of Nebraska–Lincoln Marketplace (Nebraska), University of Puget Sound (Washington), University of Texas El Paso Geological Sciences Department (Texas), University of Washington (Washington), U.S. Geological Survey (District of Columbia), UT News: The University of Texas at Austin (Texas), Vanderbilt University (Tennessee), Visit Dallas (Texas), Weatherford Democrat (Texas), Western Science Center (California), West Philly Local (Pennsylvania), Westword (Colorado), White Mountain Independent (Arizona), Woodlands Online (Texas), and Xavier Newswire (Kentucky).

Earth Science Week also was covered by **television and radio stations** across the country, including 97.9 WHAV (Massachusetts), ABC News 4 (South Carolina), b93.fm (Canada), FOX 47 News (Michigan), I-100 Iconic Rock (New York), iradiophilly (Pennsylvania), KALW Local Public Radio (California), KEVN Black Hills FOX (South Dakota), KFVS 12 (Missouri), KFYR News (North Dakota), KOLD News 13 (Arizona), KSIS Radio (Missouri), KX News (North Dakota), KY3 (Missouri), Wane 15 News (Indiana), WCSC News 5 (South Carolina), WHCU Radio (New York), WJON AM 1240 FM 95.3 (Minnesota), WKU Public Radio (Kentucky), WNKY 40 News (Kentucky), WTNH News 8 (Connecticut), and WTVQ 36 News (Kentucky).

AGI distributed **press releases** to hundreds of newspapers, magazines, and other print media outlets. The articles highlighted Earth Science Week activities and the program theme. Press releases about Earth Science Week activities were also released by AGI, Coffee County News, EIN Presswire, Lewis County Herald, and SVI News.

Copies of the **Earth Science Week 2020 poster,** featuring a geoscience learning activity in addition to promotional content, were distributed as inserts in publications carrying articles about the event, such as NESTA's The Earth Scientist, GSA Today, and AAPG Explorer,. In addition, the poster image appeared in the Society of Exploration Geoscientists' The Leading Edge and Nautilus magazine.

Earth Science Week Sponsors

United States Geological Survey

National Aeronautics and Space Administration

National Park Service

American Association of Petroleum Geologists Foundation

American Geophysical Union

Geothermal Resources Council

IF/THEN® (Lyda Hill Philanthropies)

Society for Mining, Metallurgy, and Exploration (Minerals Education Coalition)

Society of Exploration Geophysicists

AmericaView

Geological Society of America

Consumer Energy Alliance

Nautilus

Water Footprint Calculator/Grace Communications Foundation

American Meteorological Society

CLEAN (Climate Literacy and Energy Awareness Network)

Global Sponsors

International Raw Materials Observatory

American Association of Petroleum Geologists Foundation

ExxonMobil

Newmont Corporation

Earth Science Week Program Partners

American Association of Petroleum Geologists

American Association of Petroleum Geologists Foundation

American Geophysical Union

American Geosciences Institute

American Institute of Professional Geologists

American Meteorological Society

AmericaView

Archaeological Institute of America

Association for Women Geoscientists

Association of American State Geologists

CLEAN (Climate Literacy and Energy Awareness Network)

Consumer Energy Alliance

Critical Zones Observatories

ExxonMobil

Geological Institute of America

Geological Society of America

Geothermal Resources Council

IF/THEN® (Lyda Hill Philanthropies)

Incorporated Research Institutions for Seismology

International Raw Materials Observatory

Mineralogical Society of America

Minerals Education Coalition

National Earth Science Teachers Association

Nautilus

Newmont Corporation

Nutrients for Life Foundation

Society for Mining, Metallurgy, and Exploration

Society of Exploration Geophysicists

Soil Science Society of America

UNAVCO

U.S. Bureau of Land Management

U.S. Forest Service

U.S. Geological Survey

U.S. National Aeronautics and Space Administration

U.S. National Oceanographic and Atmospheric Administration

U.S. National Park Service

U.S. National Science Foundation

Water Footprint Calculator/Grace Communications Foundation

Earth Science Week 2020 Events and Activities by State and Territory

While it is impossible to track all Earth Science Week activities in the United States, major activities across the country included:

Alabama

- The governor of Alabama issued a proclamation for Earth Science Week 2020.
- The National Speleological Society and the Geological Survey of Alabama distributed complimentary Earth Science Week Toolkits to science educators for use in the classroom.
- The Geological Survey of Alabama promoted participation in Earth Science Week 2020 on its website as well as through its social media platforms.
- The University of South Alabama Archaeology Museum welcomed visitors of all ages to participate virtually in International Archaeology Day on October 17.
- For National Fossil Day 2020, the Huntsville Science Festival hosted a virtual talk with paleontologist and author Dr. Scott Persons. Persons discussed the discovery of Scotty, the largest *T. rex* ever discovered. He also presented evidence revealing what life was like for this amazing dinosaur.
- The University of Alabama's Museum of Natural History, in partnership with the Geological Survey of Alabama, hosted a free National Fossil Day livestream event celebrating fossil appreciation and stewardship.
- The Anniston Museum and the Alabama Paleontological Society Inc. were official National Fossil Day partners, this year.
- Birmingham Paleontological Society promoted the virtual National Fossil Day events held by the Alabama Museum of Natural History in Tuscaloosa, Alabama.
- The Center for Archaeological Studies and the University's Archaeology Museum presented a virtual preview of their exhibit, scheduled to open in the Fall of 2021, just in time for International Archaeology Day 2020.

Alaska

- The governor of Alaska issued a perpetual proclamation of Earth Science Week.
- Alaska's Division of Geological and Geophysical Surveys, the Alaska Museum of Natural History, and the University of Alaska Museum of the North were official National Fossil Day partners in 2020.
- The Alaska National Parks promoted participation in Earth Science Week 2020 on their website, especially National Fossil Day, as well as through social media.

Arizona

- Grand Canyon National Park hosted multiple virtual events for the 11th annual National Fossil Day celebration. Activities included a ranger-led virtual visit to a 270 million-year-old marine fossil bed, a behind-the-scenes look at the park's Museum Collection to examine Ice Age fossils and trilobites, and evening lectures.
- The Arizona Geological Survey, Arizona Science Center, and the Southwest Paleontological Society were among the 2020 list of National Fossil Day partners.
- Arizona State University promoted National Fossil Day 2020 online by gathering an electronic collection of some of the world's more unusual fossils from the university scientists who study them.
- Visitors were invited to celebrate International Archaeology Day at the Pueblo Grande Museum, Phoenix's only preserved archaeological site, on October 20. Archaeology aficionados of all ages witnessed preservation techniques on the prehistoric platform mound, participated in a simulated archaeological dig, and did hands-on crafts inspired by archaeology and southwestern cultures. Visitors were also invited attend a free lecture by archaeologist and author Dr. Glen Rice on altruism in food sharing among the 19th Century O'odham.
- The Museum of Northern Arizona virtually shared a fossil, recently donated to the museum, with the public in honor of National Fossil Day.
- The Pinal Gem and Mineral Society held its October meeting, which included a fossil exhibit in celebration of National Fossil Day, at the Pinal Geology and Mineral Museum.
- Events were offered to the public for National Fossil Day at Petrified Forest National Park. The in-person event included activities at the Museum Demonstration Lab, plus a Paleontology Video Series with park paleontologists streamed on YouTube.
- For National Fossil Day, the Arizona Museum of Natural History invited guests to celebrate America's paleontological heritage with activities, facts, and artwork, including a 40-page downloadable coloring book.
- Verde Valley Archaeology Center's International Archaeology Day gala, held virtually this year, celebrated both International Archaeology Day and the center's 10th anniversary.
- Just in time for National Fossil Day, Petrified Forest National Park announced that park visitors could, once again, talk with a park paleontologist while they work on fossils in the demonstration fossil laboratory. To ensure safety and social distancing, two-way radios were used for communication while the paleontologists and fossils were made viewable through the laboratory window.

Arkansas

- The Arkansas Archeological Survey created, and shared on its YouTube channel, videos introducing the public to the survey in honor of International Archaeology Day.
- The Arkansas Geological Survey, the Arkansas Museum of Discovery, and the Pratt Museum were among partners celebrating National Fossil Day this year.

California

- Finalists in the Earth Science Week photography contest included Ella Giguere of San Carlos, California, and Tori Judy of Belmont, California.
- Shreya Dhanala of Folsom, California, was a finalist in this year's Earth Science Week video contest.
- The Western Science Center celebrated National Fossil Day virtually with free, downloadable activities developed by their museum educators.
- The University of California Museum of Paleontology promoted National Fossil Day 2020 on its website, sharing an electronic collection of fossils, including the fossilized tooth whorl of *Helicoprion*, a shark relative that lived during the Permian about 298–252 million years ago.
- The California Geological Survey, Anza-Borrego Desert State Park, Children's Discovery Museum of San Jose, Fossil Discovery Center of Madera County, and the Page Museum at La Brea Tar Pits were National Fossil Day partners.
- The California Department of Conservation promoted Earth Science Week 2020 on its website, including daily blog posts for each Focus Day.
- The Raymond M. Alf Museum of Paleontology, the Natural History Museum of Los Angeles County's Invertebrate Paleontology Department, and the San Bernardino County Museum held virtual museum tours on October 14 in celebration of National Fossil Day.

- UCLA's Cotsen Institute of Archaeology celebrated archaeology throughout October by compiling a collection of resources and events to show the public what archaeology is about. Guests explored everything from international excavations to the details found under microscopes in labs. In addition, an online lecture series was offered on Wednesdays throughout the month.
- The Western Science Center virtually celebrated International Archaeology Day with "Science Saturday" including free, downloadable activities developed by museum educators and Mt. San Jacinto College Anthropology students.
- KALW Local Public Radio highlighted National Fossil Day, a focus day of Earth Science Week, on its website.

Colorado

- For Geologic Map Day, Meta County Women's Social, Adventure, and Hiking Group offered a guided hike through Devil's Canyon, where attendees learned how to read a geologic map and use a Brunton compass in the field.
- Participants joined Bureau of Land Management geologist Eric Eckberg on a guided talk through Devil's Canyon for Geologic Map Day.
- The Minerals Education Coalition promoted Earth Science Week and Focus Days such as the inaugural Minerals Day event on its website.
- The Museums of Western Colorado hosted a National Fossil Day virtual talk with Curator of Paleontology Dr. Julia McHugh in which she showed the unique fossils stored in the Dinosaur Journey collections. The museums also sponsored a virtual talk on "A Historyography of Rock Art" for International Archaeology Day. Tabitha McFarland gave a museums' virtual talk on her "accidental path" to paleontology in honor of Geoscience for Everyone Day.

- The Western Interior Paleontological Society promoted public participation in National Fossil Day.
- Royal Gorge Regional Museum and History Center hosted an activity pick-up day to celebrate National Fossil Day. Children's activities were made available on October 10th.
- The Colorado University Museum of Natural History invited the public to join in celebrating National Fossil Day.
- The Colorado Geological Survey, Friends of Dinosaur Ridge, Garden Park Fossil Area, Denver Museum of Nature and Science, Rocky Mountain Dinosaur Resource Center, Morrison Natural History Museum, and the Rocky Mountain Association of Geologists were partners in National Fossil Day.
- The Roxborough State Park, the Lamb Spring Archaeology Preserve, and the Bradford House in Ken Caryl hosted guests celebrating International Archaeology Day. Events included a "Walk Through Time" poster exhibit, a lecture, the "Archaeological Walk and Talk" program, an archaeology exhibit, and a Zoom panel discussion.
- Florissant Fossil Beds National Monument promoted the celebration of National Fossil Day.
- The Garden of the Gods Visitor & Nature Center hosted a free family fun day with partners offering educational presentations, fossil identification, hands-on activities, and more.
- Earth Science Week 2020 Toolkits were distributed to students, teachers, and others by representatives of the American Institute of Professional Geologists, the Society of Economic Geologists, the National Earth Science Teachers Association, and the Geological Society of America.
- A series of events, co-sponsored by Colorado Parks and Wildlife and Roxborough State Park, were held throughout October, with a guided activity almost every day

of the month. The program featured guided tours, hikes, walks, lectures, and more.

Connecticut

- International Archaeology Day was celebrated at the Institute for American Indian Studies. Guests were invited to dig into the fun with staff and uncover what makes archaeology a fascinating field of study.
- The Connecticut Department of Energy and Environmental Protection promoted Earth Science Week by distributing educational materials.
- Yale Peabody Museum of Natural History promoted the celebration of National Fossil Day by showcasing the Permian reefs in the Guadalupe and Glass Mountains of west Texas.
- The Connecticut Geological Survey, Dinosaur (Trackways) State Park, Bruce Museum, and New Haven Mineral Club were National Fossil Day partners.

Delaware

- The governor of Delaware issued a perpetual proclamation of Earth Science Week.
- Ohioans joined the ODNR Division of Geological Survey in celebrating the state's natural history during Earth Science Week. To accommodate restrictions on large gatherings during pandemic, geologists and special guests presented several free webinars on a variety of topics.
- The Delaware Geological Survey promoted Earth Science Week and Geologic Map Day by distributing Earth Science Week Toolkits and informational materials to educators. In addition, the survey promoted Earth Science Week online.
- The Delaware Museum of Natural History and Delaware Geological Survey were partners of this year's National Fossil Day celebration.

District of Columbia

- Numerous federal agencies, including the U.S. Geological Survey, NASA, and the National Park Service, supported Earth Science Week with the provision of teaching materials, distribution of kits, and events and activities.
- During National Fossil Day events held across the country, the National Park Service offered young people a chance to download the Junior Paleontologist activity booklet off its website.
- The Geological Society of America encouraged geocachers around the world to participate in International EarthCache Day during Earth Science Week.
- The U.S. Geological Survey encouraged people around the world to participate in Earth Science Week by highlighting activities relating to Focus Days of Earth Science Week online.
- The Natural Science Collections Alliance promoted National Fossil Day online.
- The Geological Society of Washington and National Environmental Education Foundation were among the D.C.-based National Fossil Day partners.
- For National Fossil Day, the Smithsonian's National Museum of Natural History held a virtual scavenger hunt live stream. Guests digitally raced through the museum's Deep Time exhibit, where their knowledge was put to the test by Smithsonian paleontologist Dr. Matthew Carrano.

Florida

- The Florida Geological Survey promoted Earth Science Week by distributing educational materials.
- Chiefland Citizen highlighted the celebration of Earth Science Week on its website.
- The Florida Geological Survey, Florida Museum of Natural History, Jacksonville Museum of Science and History, Mulberry Phosphate Museum, Orlando Science Center, South Florida Museum, Frost Museum of Science, Florida Paleontological Society, Florida Fossil Hunters, and Manasota Fossil Club were National Fossil Day partners.
- In celebration of National Fossil Day, the Phillip and Patricia Frost Museum of Science held the second season of its Virtual LIVE@Frost Science speaker series.
- Rachel Xu of Gainesville, Florida, was selected as a finalist in this years' Earth Science Week essay contest.
- The Florida Department of the Geological celebrated Earth Science Week by inviting the public to join state geologist Jon Arthur in learning how Earth sciences influence our daily lives and the future.
- The Florida Geological Survey promoted Earth Science Week Photography, Video, Essay and Visual Arts contests on its website.
- Florida's Bishop Museum of Science and Nature hosted a National Fossil Day event where visitors practiced their paleontology skills and learned about Florida's fossil history.
- The Florida Public Archaeology Network and the Charlotte County Libraries and History Division hosted a local event in honor of International Archaeology Day to connect Southwest Florida with its long human history which reaches back thousands of years. This online event offered information on local heritage sites, archaeology-themed crafts, and presentations by renowned archaeologists discussing the unique archaeology of Florida.

Georgia

- Justin Xu of Sugar Hill, Georgia, won first place in the visual arts contest with a creative and colorful drawing that included the many ways Earth materials are used.
- Fernbank Science Center and Georgia Southern University Museum were National Fossil Day partners.

• Elizabeth Xu was recognized as a finalist in Earth Science Week's visual arts contest.
• Tellus Science Museum sponsored a monthly online event to celebrate National Fossil Day in which participants quizzed knowledgeable staff.

Hawaii
• Lyman Museum and Mission House was a National Fossil Day partner.

Idaho
• In honor of Geologic Map Day, the Idaho Geological Survey shared its geologic map of the Crane Creek Reservoir Quadrangle in Washington County online.
• Idaho Museum of Natural History promoted National Fossil Day through its social media platforms, inviting the public to get the program coloring book available on the National Park Service website.
• Hagerman Fossil Beds National Monument promoted National Fossil Day 2020 online, gathering an electronic collection of their Hagerman horse fossils as well as a providing a link to pages from a prehistoric life coloring book.
• A celebration of National Fossil Day and Earth Science Week was held at the Idaho Museum of Mining and Geology in collaboration with the Orma J. Smith Museum of Natural History. Visitors explored activities about Idaho's geology, fossils, and dinosaurs.

Illinois
• The governor of Illinois issued a perpetual proclamation of Earth Science Week.
• Akhshith Rengaraju of Aurora, Illinois, won first place in the Earth Science Week essay contest with the paper on "Our Next Step."
• The Chicago Society of the Archaeological Institute of America sponsored an interactive and safe challenge to celebrate International Archaeology Day and the material culture and history of Chicagoland.
• Augustana College's Fryxell Geology Museum, the Field Museum, Burpee Museum of Natural History, Children's Discovery Museum, the Peggy Notebaert Natural History Museum, and the Southern Illinois Earth Science Club were partners for National Fossil Day.
• In celebration of National Fossil Day, the Illinois State Museum hosted a virtual event where viewers examined the Illinois State Museum's Paleontology Collection with curator Melissa Pardi.
• The Earth Science Club of Northern Illinois promoted participation in National Fossil Day on its website.
• The Southern Illinois University Edwardsville STEM Center encouraged community members to take part in an outdoor learning opportunity by visiting EarthCache sites on the SIUE campus and in the region.
• The Naperville Park District promoted participation in National Fossil Day on its website.
• During Earth Science Week, the Gazette-Democrat noted National Fossil Day, which "was celebrated around the world and throughout the universe on October 14th with parades, hoopla and lots of other exciting activities."

Indiana
• Indiana Geological Survey, Indianapolis's Children's Museum, Indiana State Museum, Joseph Moore Museum of Natural History, WonderLab Museum of Science, and Indiana's Earth Science Teachers Association were National Fossil Day partners.
• Fox Island County Park welcomed guests of all ages to spend National Fossil Day digging up different rocks and artifacts they found in the park. Any treasures discovered during the event were "finders' keepers."
• Falls of the Ohio Foundation hosted guests to celebrate National Fossil Day at the Falls of the Ohio State Park with a series of special fossil bed hikes, reduced adult admission for their Interpretive Center, guides on the collecting piles, and more.
• Members of the public to met at the Nature Center of Clifty Falls State Park to embark on a fossil hike to discuss and explore deep time.

Iowa
• Iowa View encouraged people of all ages to participate in Earth Science Week by highlighting the Focus Days of Earth Science Week on its website.
• The Buchanan County Conservation Board sponsored Fossil Fun Day, allowing attendees to explore Buchanan County Park while discovering Iowa's paleontological past.
• Iowa's partners for Nation Fossil Day included the Devonian Fossil Gorge, Fossil and Prairie Center, Sanford Museum and Planetarium, University of Iowa's Museum of Natural History, and the Mid-America Paleontology Society.

Kansas
• The Kansas Geological Survey distributed Earth Science Week Toolkits for educators.
• Fort Hays State University's Department of Geosciences hosted virtual events, activities, and contests throughout October celebrating Earth Science Week.
• El Quartelejo Museum in Scott City, Kansas, celebrated National Fossil Day by recommending activities, such as the National Fossil Day Art Contest, for participants of all ages.
• Scientists and students from the University of Kansas' Biodiversity Institute and the Natural History Museum welcomed guests joining them for a virtual paleontology party on October 14. New videos were released at the top of each hour.

- Sternberg Museum of Natural History hosted guests virtually for exclusive content on October 14 to celebrate National Fossil Day.
- Among the list of National Fossil Day partners were the Kansas Geological Survey, Fick Fossil and History Museum, and Prairie Oaks Nature Center.

Kentucky

- The Kentucky Geological Survey virtually hosted its annual Open House to celebrate Earth Science Week. The survey also offered an Earth Science Week webpage with short videos about geology and geologists; information about rocks, minerals, and fossils; and links to home-based science activities.
- Friends of Big Bone Lick promoted participation in National Fossil Day through social media platforms.
- The Kentucky Geological Survey distributed kits among educators in celebration of Earth Science Week.
- For National Fossil Day, Mammoth Cave National Park shared news about the trove of shark fossils found deep in the passageways of Mammoth Cave.
- Big Bone Lick State Historic Site and Kentucky Paleontological Society were National Fossil Day partners.

Louisiana

- The Audubon Nature Institute was a partner of this year's National Fossil Day celebration.

Maine

- Archelaus Paxon of El Paso, Texas, was selected as a finalist in this year's Earth Science Week essay contest.
- The Maine Geological Survey and the L.C. Bates Museum were partners for National Fossil Day.

Maryland

- The Maryland Geological Survey distributed kits among educators in celebration of Earth Science Week.
- Chesapeake Children's Museum hosted Fossil Day, an all-day event of dinosaur facts and fun for all ages at the Calvert Marine Museum.
- Maryland's Dinosaur Park and the Maryland Science Center were National Fossil Day partners.
- The Calvert Marine Museum held a virtual museum tour on October 14 in celebration of National Fossil Day.

Massachusetts

- The American Meteorological Society distributed complimentary Earth Science Week Toolkits to science educators.
- Buttonwoods Museum held a virtual Archaeology Open House to celebrate Massachusetts Archaeology Month and International Archaeology Day. Featured artifacts included lithics, steatite bowl fragments and ceramic fragments that span the ancient occupational period of Native Americans in the area. Archaeology volunteer Nancy Lebar described the uses of these artifacts and the people who made and used them in their lives along the Merrimack River.
- For National Fossil Day, the Harvard Museum of Natural History welcomed visitors to virtually meet Harvard paleontologists through a series of four free webinars on the prehistoric animals on exhibit.
- Lowell National Historical Park sponsored an International Archaeology Day walking tour of standing structures and the landscape of Boott Cotton Mills.

Michigan

- Jessica Malkin of Grand Rapids, Michigan, was selected as a finalist in the 2020 Earth Science Week photography contest.
- Canton Public Library promoted Earth Science Week on its website.
- The Marquette Regional History Center presented "Archaeology Bingo Scavenger Hunt" throughout October in celebration of International Archaeology Day.
- University of Michigan Museum of Natural History, Michigan's Mineralogical Society, as well as the Michigan Earth Science Teachers Association were National Fossil Day partners.
- The Michigan State University Museum hosted a poetry session with Jay Artemis Hull, a Michigan-based poet who draws inspiration from fossils, rocks, and nature.
- Michigan State University Museum hosted the first-ever Virtual MSU Federal Credit Union Dinosaur Dash on October 4–10. Participants submitted virtual times, downloaded finisher's certificates, and uploaded photos from their virtual activities.
- The Marquette Regional History Center presented "Archaeology Bingo Scavenger Hunt" in celebration of the 10th anniversary of International Archaeology Day.
- Michigan Technological University hosted a series of virtual career day events in September as part of its Career FEST. Students learned about job and career opportunities.
- Sherry Claflin, an eighth-grade Earth science teacher at White Cloud Junior High School in White Cloud, Michigan, won the Edward C. Roy Jr. Award for Excellence in K–8 Earth Science Teaching. Claflin received the award, given annually by AGI, in April at the virtual National Earth Science Teachers Association's Friends of Earth Science Reception.
- The University of Michigan Museum of Paleontology held a virtual museum tour on October 14 to celebrate National Fossil Day

Minnesota

- The Minnesota Geological Survey and the National Association of Geoscience Teachers promoted Earth Science Week among teachers and citizens.
- WJON AM 1240 FM 93.5 shared a news post about the importance of the geosciences and "Earth Materials in Our Lives" in honor of Earth Science Week's 2020 theme.
- The Minnesota Geological Survey, Duluth Children's Museum, Science Museum of Minnesota, and the Geological Society of Minnesota were National Fossil Day partners.
- Carleton College promoted Earth Science Week on the SERC-Carlton website.

Mississippi

- For Earth Science Week, Mississippi State College of Arts & Sciences highlighted a week's worth of events, including a National Fossil Day video series.
- Dunn-Seiler Museum and the Department of Geosciences at Mississippi State University celebrated National Fossil Day with a video series called "Paleo Perspectives: Becoming a Paleontologist." In the series, paleontologists from around the country shared stories of scientific discovery and talked about their paths to careers in paleontology.
- Mississippi Petrified Forest was a National Fossil Day partner.

Missouri

- The governor of Missouri recognized October 11–17 as Earth Science Week.
- The Missouri Department of Natural Resources promoted Earth Science Week among teachers and citizens with the distribution of educational materials.
- The Bollinger County Museum of Natural History held an International Archaeology Day and National Fossil Day celebration in Marble Hill, Missouri, on October 10. Children's activities included a children's fossil dig, dinosaur dig, and fossil scavenger hunt. Children were also able to pick up a free activity kit containing archaeology and fossil games and puzzles.
- The Mastodon State Historic Park, Missouri's Institute of Natural Science, and the St. Louis Science Center were National Fossil Day partners.
- Missouri State Geography, Geology, and Planning Associate Professor Dr. Gary Michelfelder shared Earth Science Week insights in a blog post.
- The Missouri Department of Natural Resources promoted participation in Earth Science Week's Focus Days and contests.
- Millions of people participated in the "Drop, Cover, and Hold On" earthquake drill on October 15 during Earth Science Week.
- Visitors to the Missouri State Museum during Earth Science Week, and especially on National Fossil Day, saw fossils in the limestone walls, floors, and stairs of the State Capitol.
- Citizens visited the Ed Clark Museum of Missouri Geology on October 11–17 to celebrate Earth Science Week.

Montana

- The University of Montana's Paleontology Center held a virtual museum tour on October 14 in celebration of National Fossil Day.
- The Fort Peck Interpretive Center and Museum, Great Plains Dinosaur Museum and Field House, and the Two Medicine Dinosaur Center were partners for National Fossil Day.
- Makoshika State Park, in partnership with the Glendive Dinosaur and Fossil Museum, held a National Fossil Day event.
- In celebration of National Fossil Day and Montana's rich fossil history, guests at the Museum of the Rockies ordered Paper Bag Paleontology, a take-home activity. Each activity bag included a mystery animal's "fossils" (made of paper) from the Jurassic period.
- Bighorn Basin Paleontological Institute organized a virtual celebration in honor of National Fossil Day 2020.

Nebraska

- The Nebraska School of Natural Resources distributed Earth Science Week educational materials.
- University of Nebraska-Lincoln promoted Earth Science Week among teachers and citizens with the distribution of educational materials.
- Omaha's Children's Museum and Ashfall Fossil Beds State Park were partners for National Fossil Day.
- University of Nebraska State Museum welcomed children and families to celebrate National Fossil Day at their special paleontology-themed Night at Morrill Hall. The event featured activities led by state museum paleontologists, where visitors could learn what a fossil is, dig and sort for fossils, and find out about sister museum Ashfall Fossil Beds State Historical Park.

Nevada

- The governor of Nevada issued a perpetual proclamation of Earth Science Week.
- The Nevada Bureau of Mines and Geology sponsored a virtual field trip, touring the natural history and geological resources in the northern Hot Springs Mountains of west-central Nevada, to celebrate Earth Science Week.
- Ice Age Fossils State Park hosted virtual events October 12–16 for National Fossil Day.
- For National Fossil Day 2020, Tule Springs Fossil Bed National Monument hosted a virtual presentation by paleontologist Eric Scott titled

"Through the Desert on a Horse with No Name." This talk focused on Pleistocene fossil horses, including research on horse fossils from Tule Springs Fossil Beds.

- The Nevada Bureau of Mines and Geology promoted awareness of Earth Science Week through its website and by distributing educational materials.
- An International Archaeology Day scavenger hunt was hosted by the Lost City Museum.

New Hampshire

- The New Hampshire Geological Survey promoted awareness of Earth Science Week among residents and community members.

New Jersey

- The New Jersey Geological and Water Survey promoted Earth Science Week and provided teachers with Earth Science Week Toolkits.
- The New Jersey State Museum hosted members of the public virtually celebrating International Archaeology Day. This online event included activities such as artifact identification, pottery reconstruction, a personal time capsule, and more. The museum also promoted participation in National Fossil Day by highlighting the event on social media.
- The Big Brook Preserve hosted an interactive fossil hunt for all ages. Participants waded the shallow waters of Big Brook and sifted through the substrate for fossils including shark teeth.
- Rowan University's Jean & Ric Edelman Fossil Park offered educational content on its website and social media pages for National Fossil Day.
- Rutgers Geology Museum's "Virtual Dinosaurs Late Night" enabled participants to step back in time to discover dinosaurs and other creatures from the Paleozoic, Mesozoic, and Cenozoic Eras. This free, online

event included do-at-home educational activities, a trivia game, and a guest presentation about Theropod dinosaurs.

New Mexico

- The New Mexico Bureau of Geology and Mineral Resources continued its 11-year tradition of hosting Earth Science week podcasts for the local public radio station on each evening of the week-long celebration.
- The New Mexico Museum of Natural History & Science hosted a National Fossil Day event touring the museum's Collections Building where an extensive catalog of fossils are kept.
- The Las Cruces Museum of Nature & Science offered families takeout STEM activity kits and several events throughout the month of October to celebrate Earth Science Week.
- For International Archaeology Day, the Office of Archaeological Studies premiered the video "Making and Breaking Pots: Summer Camp in the Box 2020."
- The Museum of Indian Arts and Culture's Archaeological Research Collections Staff at the Center for New Mexico Archaeology hosted an "Ask an Archaeologist" event on October 24 to celebrate International Archaeology Month.
- The Las Cruces Museum of Nature and Science and the Bureau of Land Management held a National Fossil Day event where visitors picked up a Fossil Day gift bag with posters, stickers, and Junior Ranger activities to do at home.
- The New Mexico Bureau of Geology and Mineral Resources distributed Earth Science Week educational materials.
- The New Mexico Bureau of Geology and Mineral Resources celebrated Earth Science Week by hosting a virtual open house to showcase its geoscience labs and Mineral Museum.

- Ghost Ranch, Prehistoric Trackways National Monument, Mesalands Community College's Dinosaur Museum, and the New Mexico Science Teachers Association were National Fossil Day partners.

New York

- The New York Times Crossword dedicated one of its famous crossword puzzles to the celebration of Earth Science Week.
- Cornell University invited guests to join in a virtual "Fossil Mania" event. The Museum of the Earth held a virtual live program, broadcast from the museum's prep lab, to celebrate fossils.
- The American Museum of Natural History and NASA@MyLibrary organized a live OpenSpace flight webcast for Earth Science Week, providing a view of Earth from satellites and showing how the ecological system is divided into major life zones.
- The Rochester Museum & Science Center and the Archaeological Institute of America's Rochester Society presented a family-friendly introduction to archaeology in honor of International Archaeology Day.
- The partners of National Fossil Day included New York's Penn Dixie Paleontological and Outdoor Education Center, Buffalo Science Museum, Science Museum of Long Island, and Warthin Museum of Natural History.
- On October 18, the Archaeological Institute of America's Rochester Society and the Cumming Nature Center hosted a public archaeological dig for families wishing to experience real-life archaeology.
- The American Museum of Natural History held virtual National Fossil Day-inspired events to help students understand how studying fossils teaches us about the history of life, past climates, and ancient landscapes. The day consisted of activities such as the exploration of

fossil formation, extinction theories, and fossil diversity.
- The Paleontological Research Institute's Museum of the Earth hosted a virtual National Fossil Day event.

North Carolina
- The North Carolina Geological Survey promoted awareness of Earth Science Week among residents and community members.
- For Earth Science Week and this year's theme of "Earth Materials in Our Lives," North Carolina Museum of Natural Sciences' Dr. Chris Tacker wrote about the importance of scientific literacy and "understanding where stuff comes from."
- The Aurora Fossil Museum celebrated National Fossil Day with a virtual fossil hunt with museum educator Dr. George Oliver. The free annual event was offered in partnership with the National Park Service.
- The North Carolina Fossil Club promoted National Fossil Day on its social media platforms, gathering activities and events happening virtually and in the surrounding areas.
- Appalachian State University's McKinney Geology Teaching Museum and North Carolina's Museum of Life and Science were National Fossil Day partners.
- North Carolina Museum of Natural Sciences' "Wednesday's Lunch Time Discovery" coincided with this year's National Fossil Day event, as the public was invited to attend "The End of the World: An Introduction to the End-Permian Mass Extinction" with Christian Kammerer, research curator of paleontology. This event was sponsored by the state Office of Environmental Education and Public Affairs and the Museum of Natural Sciences.
- In honor of National Fossil Day, Discovery Place Science Museum enabled guests to learn about what fossils are and how they are created.

- North Carolina's Museum of Natural Sciences promoted Earth Science Week, highlighting Minerals Day as the newest Focus Day on its website.
- Imagination Station Science and History Museum hosted a National Fossil Day-inspired event including activities focusing on fossils.
- Environmental Education in North Carolina promoted Earth Science Week among teachers and citizens.
- Asheville Museum of Science offered STEM Lab Activities for Earth Science Week. Live science demonstrations on erosion, runoff, sediment pollution, and the water cycle ran throughout the day.
- For Earth Science Week, Concord University's Environmental Geosciences program and the North Carolina Geological Survey co-hosted a live online presentation about the summer earthquake near Sparta, North Carolina.

North Dakota
- North Dakota's governor issued a perpetual proclamation of Earth Science Week.
- Everett Lee of Fargo, North Dakota, was selected as a finalist of Earth Science Week's visual arts contest.
- North Dakota's Geological Survey promoted National Fossil Day on its website.
- The Dakota Science Center, North Dakota Geological Survey, and North Dakota Geological Society were partners for National Fossil Day.

Ohio
- The Ohio Division of Geological Survey promoted Earth Science Week and ways to get involved on its website.
- One of the individuals selected as a finalist in the Earth Science Week essay contest is Clara Zabik of Chagrin Falls, Ohio.
- Ohioans were welcomed by the School of Earth Sciences and the

Orton Geological Museum in celebrating Earth Science Week and National Fossil Day. The celebration was completely virtual, with an installation of a Digital Exhibit of Ohio fossils, a new video, and a live talk.
- The Ohio Department of Natural Resources Division of the Geological Survey and the Ohio Earth Science Teachers Association distributed Earth Science Week Toolkits and other materials.
- The Falls of the Ohio State Park celebrated National Fossil Day with a series of fossil bed hikes, reduced adult admission for the Interpretive Center, guides on the collecting piles, and talks and displays about fossils.
- To celebrate archaeology and its contributions to society, Ohio History Connection put together a series of sessions dedicated to planning International Archaeology Day events.
- The Ohio Division of Geological Survey celebrated Earth Science Week with free webinars enabling Ohioans to discover the Earth sciences and engage in stewardship of our planet.
- In celebration of National Fossil Day, Ohio State University and the Ohio Geological Survey ran an online presentation about fossils in Columbus Limestone.

Oklahoma
- Oklahoma's governor issued a perpetual proclamation of Earth Science Week.
- Spiro Mounds Archaeological Center celebrated International Archaeology Day with a lecture, a guided walk, and other activities. Oklahoma Archaeology Month, sponsored by the Oklahoma Anthropological Society and the Oklahoma Public Archaeology Network, included more events throughout October.
- Sam Noble Museum celebrated National Fossil Day highlighting

the *Cotylorhynchus* fossil on social media. Visitors viewed a replica of the *Cotylorhynchus* in their newest exhibit, "Permian Monsters: Life Before the Dinosaurs," and saw its skeleton in the Ancient Life Gallery. The museum also hosted a re-watch of the Hidden Gallery Gem episode featuring the *Cotylorhynchus*.

• The Oklahoma Geological Survey, the Association of Environmental & Engineering Geologists, the Society for Sedimentary Geology, and the American Association of Petroleum Geologists distributed Earth Science Week Toolkits to educators and students.

Oregon

• Achyut Balaji of Hillsboro, Oregon, was a finalist in the 2020 Earth Science Week video contest.

• On October 14, a free live online discussion was held with local amateur paleontologist Greg Carr, a longtime volunteer with the Rice Museum and a member of the North American Research Group of amateur paleontologists who scour sedimentary rocks across the western U.S. for fossil remains. As a fossil preparation expert, Carr gave a tour of his home lab and talked through the process of how to carefully remove rock to expose the fossil within.

• The governor of Oregon issued a proclamation for Earth Science Week 2020.

• The John Day Fossil Beds National Monument premiered a new National Fossil Day virtual video tour of collections on its website and social media accounts. The focus was non-mammal fossils that can be found in the fossil gallery at the Thomas Condon Paleontology and Visitor Center.

• National Fossil Day partners included Oregon's Department of Geology and Mineral Industries and Douglas County Museum of Natural and Cultural History.

• The University of Oregon Museum of Natural and Cultural History celebrated National Fossil Day a virtual investigation of fossils. Guests joined online for the museum's Little Wonders program, featuring stories, hands-on activities, and more.

Pennsylvania

• The staff of the Penn State Earth & Mineral Sciences Museum and Art Gallery promoted Earth Science Week through its website and social media. They also provided several educational videos on their YouTube channel.

• The Pennsylvania Public Library for Union County encouraged people of all ages to celebrate Earth Science Week by exploring Pennsylvania's caverns and caves, virtually or in person, and entering a contest.

• On National Fossil Day, the State Museum of Pennsylvania offered young people a chance to explore pre-historic animals that lived before, with, and after the dinosaurs by downloading a word search from the website.

• For International Archaeology Day, the Penn Museum and the Academy of Natural Sciences virtually co-hosted "Ask the Scientists: Ancient '-Ologies'," a fun, interactive program in which children lead the conversation.

• Pennsylvania's Geological Survey, Ferncliff Peninsula Natural Area, Carnegie Science Center, Reading Public Museum, Pennsylvania Earth Science Teachers Association, and the Delaware Valley Paleontological Society were National Fossil Day partners.

• World-renowned Carnegie Museum of Natural History paleontologist, Matt Lamanna, discussed dinosaur fossils presently in the lab for National Fossil Day.

• Penn Dixie Fossil Park & Nature Reserve promoted Earth Science Week on social media, including daily posts for each Focus Day.

• Drexel University's Academy of Natural Sciences invited guests to talk to a scientist, practice paleontology in The Big Dig, check out the Fossil Prep Lab to see real dinosaur bones being excavated and prepared, and more.

• In time for International Archaeology Day, the Penn Museum reopened to the public, providing a safe, awe-inspiring experience, with events online.

• State Museum of Pennsylvania invited the public to join in celebrating National Fossil Day.

• Guests visited Raccoon Creek State Park on National Fossil Day and learned what plants and animals used to call it home.

• Earth Science Week Toolkits were distributed statewide by the Pennsylvania Geological Survey.

• The Union County Library System of Pennsylvania helped families celebrate Earth Science Week with Earth-based activities and stickers from the library.

• The governor of Pennsylvania declared October 11–17 to be Earth Science Week.

• The Newlin Grist Mill hosted an archaeology dig for the public to celebrate International Archeology Day.

Puerto Rico

• Ciencia Puerto Rico promoted the celebration of Earth Science Week among the public.

• To help teach young people in her community about how to be prepared in the event of a hurricane, educator Lynette Alomar arranged "How Does a Tree Behave in a Hurricane?," a SEED-inspired activity for students at the Jesus M. Suarez Elementary School in Carolina, Puerto Rico.

Rhode Island

• Finalists in the Earth Science Week photography contest included Evan Costa of Chepachet, Rhode Island.

• Rhode Island's Geological Survey and Museum of Natural History and Planetarium were among this year's National Fossil Day partners.

South Carolina
• Finalists in the Earth Science Week visual arts contest included Teagin Costanzo of Mauldin, South Carolina.
• Finalists in this years' Earth Science Week video contest included Jeremiah Johnson-Reynolds of Blythewood, South Carolina.
• South Carolina's State Museum welcomed guests to a virtual fossil-themed trivia night in honor of National Fossil Day.
• The South Carolina Geological Survey distributed Earth Science Week Toolkits to educators.
• Environmental Education in South Carolina promoted Earth Science Week among teachers and citizens.
• The College of Charleston's Mace Brown Museum of Natural History unveiled a dinosaur exhibit in time for National Fossil Day. To celebrate, the museum launched videos that took viewers on a virtual guided tour through the paleontological gallery and fossil preparation laboratory.

South Dakota
• South Dakota's governor issued a perpetual proclamation of Earth Science Week.
• National Fossil Day was celebrated by the Museum of Geology at School of Mines and Technology. All week long, there were events, tours, and exhibits highlighting geology and paleontology.
• South Dakota's Mammoth Site invited the public to visit on Facebook on October 14, as science educator discussed fossil teeth and how they relate to the fossil record.

Tennessee
• The Tennessee Geological Survey distributed Earth Science Week Toolkits to educators.
• Bledsoe Creek State Park promoted several events in honor of Earth Science Week.
• East Tennessee State University's General Shale Brick Natural History Museum and Gray Fossil Site held a celebration for National Fossil Day.
• The Frank H. McClung Museum of Natural History and Culture and the Pink Palace Museum were National Fossil Day partners.
• On National Fossil Day, Gray Fossil Site invited online paleontological exploration of its Educator Resources website containing information, videos, news, and more from the distant past of East Tennessee.
• The Tennessee STEAM Festival, founded by Discovery Center, hosted virtual and hands-on workshops across the state, from scavenger hunts to ballets to hiking maps.
• Vanderbilt University hosted a free virtual National Fossil Day event for young people on October 10. The event featured paleontologists from Vanderbilt's departments of biological sciences and Earth and environmental sciences, including Larisa DeSantis, Rachel Racicot, Neil Kelley, and Simon Darroch.
• Earth Science Week at Discovery Park featured interactive programs and activities for visitors.
• International Archaeology Day events were held at the Parthenon in Nashville and at the Chucalissa in Memphis.

Texas
• The Bureau of Economic Geology held "Austin Earth Science Zoomerama 2020," a distance-learning series of video conferences using Zoom. This educational series engaged middle- and high-school students in exploring topics and careers in the geosciences. Fourteen sessions to connected students with geoscientists including geologists, hydrologists, paleontologist, petroleum exploration geologists, aerospace engineers, and meteorologists.
• The University of Texas at El Paso's Geological Sciences Department presented Earth Science Week virtual field trips, science presentations, raffles, and DIY workshops on October 16–22.
• In honor of International Archaeology Day and National Pollen Week, the Witte Museum invited guests to explore the world of archaeobotany in the 6th annual "Can You Dig It?" event.
• The Arlington Archosaur Site promoted National Fossil Day events statewide through social media.
• Mineral Wells Fossil Park celebrated National Fossil Day on October 17.
• Archaeological Institute of America's Houston Society sponsored a video taking the viewer through the steps of flintknapping.
• Dinosaur Valley State Park, Fossil Rim Wildlife Center, Ladonia Fossil Park, Centennial Museum, Heard Natural Science Museum and Wildlife Sanctuary, Mayborn Museum, Museum of Texas Tech University, Panhandle-Plains Historical Museum, Sherman Museum, East Texas Gem and Mineral Society, Paleontological Society of Austin, and the Dallas Zoo were among partners in National Fossil Day.
• The Texas Memorial Museum held a public event for National Fossil Day with activities including fossil identifications and a paleontologist meet-and-greet.
• During Earth Science Week, the 67th Annual Gem, Jewelry, Mineral & Fossil Show was hosted virtually this year by the Houston Gem & Mineral Society.
• The Mineral Wells Chamber of Commerce held its annual Crazy Fossil Dig on October 17 at Mineral Wells Fossil Park, including fossil displays and a scavenger hunt. Special guest Lee Higgenbotham, a paleontologist from Dallas, spoke of identifying fossils and the area's prehistoric times.

- Teachers celebrated National Fossil Day with rangers at Waco Mammoth National Monument. Attendees built their own classroom fossil kits, which included lesson plans to help students learn why there are no T. rexes in Central Texas.
- The Texas Memorial Museum shared fossils from its collection, along with a story time for younger viewers and a tutorial for creating a fossil with common kitchen staples.
- On social media, Whiteside Museum of Natural History highlighted a list of women paleontologists for National Fossil Day.
- For Earth Science Week, guests explored the newly reopened Perot Museum of Nature and Science.
- On October 14, the Dallas Paleontological Society sponsored eight National Fossil Day events.
- Dallas Public Library celebrated National Fossil Day by hosting visitors who joined a former National Park Service Ranger and guests from the Dallas Paleontological Society as they dug into Dallas's past to discover what life was like millions of years ago.
- The Houston Museum of Natural Science featured a Texas native, the Dimetrodon, on its social media platforms in honor of National Fossil Day.
- Earth Science Week Toolkits were distributed to students, teachers, and others by the Texas Bureau of Economic Geology and the Society of Exploration Geophysicists.
- The Houston Geological Society celebrated Earth Science Week online with links to various media on each Focus Day. The society provided links to videos, field trips, and other offerings that engaged young people and others in exploring the relationship between Earth materials and people.
- Visitors celebrated National Fossil Day at the Woodlands Children's Museum on October 14. Children got an up-close view of the museum's fossil collection and learned how a fossil is formed.

Utah

- Earth Science Week 2020 Toolkits were distributed to students, teachers, and others by the Utah Geological Survey and Utah Digital Labs.
- The fifth annual Moab Festival of Science was sponsored by the U.S. Geological Survey, Utah Department of Natural Resources, National Park Service, Department of Energy, Museum of Moab, and others. This event connected and inspired citizens of southeastern Utah with wonders of science through numerous hands-on activities and tours.
- Dinosaur National Monument virtually shared its museum collections with the public during Earth Science Week. Featured offerings included a link to search a geologic map of the state, a science-of-rocks worksheet, a view of satellite images using Landsat, and several videos showcasing museum collections.
- Utah Geological Survey, Cleveland-Lloyd Dinosaur Quarry, Ogden Eccles Dinosaur Park, St. George Dinosaur Discovery Site at Johnson Farm, Garth and Jerri Frehner Museum of Natural History, the Thanksgiving Point Museum of Ancient Life, University of Utah Natural History Museum, Utah Friends of Paleontology, and Earth Science Education were partners National Fossil Day.
- The Prehistoric Museum and the Utah Field House of Natural History State Park Museum highlighted collections of fossils from across Utah's geologic history for National Fossil Day.

Vermont

- Vermont's Geological Survey and Chazy Fossil Reef were partners for National Fossil Day.

Virginia

- Isabella Van Deman and Faith Qin of Virginia Beach, Virginia, won first place in the Earth Science Week video contest with their entry on halite, which covered historical, cultural, and scientific dimensions.
- Korina Cortezano of Virginia Beach, Virginia, was a finalist in this years' Earth Science Week essay contest.
- The National Science Foundation's Office of Legislative and Public Affairs produced a new video for Earth Science Week 2020.
- The Virginia Geological Survey, Science Museum of Virginia, Virginia Museum of Natural History, and Paleo Quest were National Fossil Day partners.
- The Virginia Museum of Natural History took part in National Fossil Day on October 13. Museum scientists displayed several large limestone slabs. Visitors helped clean these slabs in preparation for an upcoming exhibit. Visitors learned more about these specimens by visiting with scientists.
- The National Science Teaching Association promoted Earth Science Week 2020 on its website, including a feature in the October NSTA Reports on the new Earth Science Week webinar series.
- The Virginia Museum of Fine Arts, co-sponsored by the Richmond Society, held a free International Archaeology Day virtual lecture.
- Jamestown Rediscovery invited the public to join in celebrating International Archaeology Day and Virginia's Archaeology Month. Attendees toured the site with an archaeologist and visited the archaearium.
- The Frontier Culture Museum of Virginia sponsored an Archaeology Day event that included activities such as excavation in dig boxes and learning about what happens after artifacts are excavated.
- Virginia's Department of Mines, Minerals, and Energy celebrated Earth Science Week with geologists hosting virtual presentations on "Earth materials in our lives."
- The U.S. Geological Survey's Youth and Education in Science office created a webpage, linking

many USGS Earth Science Week efforts, on its website, including Focus Day "top stories," a minerals tongue-twister for kids, America-View poster downloads, and posters of artwork to highlight Earth resources in Native American artwork and textiles.

- The governor of Virginia issued a proclamation for Earth Science Week 2020.
- Earth Science Week 2020 Toolkits were distributed to students, teachers, and others by the Virginia Department of Mines, Minerals, and Energy.

Washington

- Alex Xu of Clyde Hill, Washington, won first place in the Earth Science Week photography contest with an image depicting many uses of Earth materials at the Snoqualmie Falls Hydroelectric Plant in Snoqualmie, Washington.
- Nathan Xu of Clyde Hill, Washington, was a finalist in the 2020 Earth Science Week visual arts contest.
- Ginkgo Petrified Forest State Park as well as the Stonerose Interpretive Center and Eocene Fossil Site were partners in National Fossil Day.
- In cooperation with the Departments of Classics at the University of Washington and the University of Puget Sound, the Puget Sound Society co-sponsored a line-up of lightning talks by community archaeologists.
- Washington locals celebrated the 11th anniversary of National Fossil Day on October 14 with the Burke Museum of Natural History and Culture's first Fossil Costume Contest.
- Earth Science Week Toolkits were distributed among science teachers by the Washington Geological Survey.

West Virginia

- In honor of Archaeology Day, Grave Creek Mound Archaeological Complex created a video demonstration on the art of flintknapping, with a special appearance from master flintknapper Robert Walden.
- On social media West Virginia Geological and Economic Survey shared resources, including fossils that can be found in its mini-museum and a coloring book available on the National Park Service website.
- Clay Center for Arts and Sciences was a partner for this year's National Fossil Day.

Wisconsin

- Earth Science Week 2020 Toolkits were distributed to students, teachers, and others by the Wisconsin Geological & Natural History Survey as well as the Soil Science Society of America.
- Wisconsin Geological and Natural History Survey promoted participation in Earth Science Week among teachers, and citizens through social media.
- The Dinosaur Discovery Museum and the Milwaukee Public Museum shared National Fossil Day events happening across the state through social media.
- Kenosha Public Museum invited the public to tune in for "Museum Munchkins LIVE," a special program for National Fossil Day that offered details on how to get certified as a Junior Paleontologist through the National Park Service.
- Weis Earth Science Museum shared its second virtual field trip video in celebration of National Fossil Day and as part of the Wisconsin Science Festival. In this video, the museum explored the Cambrian shorelines of Blackberry Hill and showed images of the first animals to walk on land.

Wyoming

- The Wyoming State Geological Survey disseminated Earth Science Week Toolkits among students and educators statewide.

- For National Fossil Day, Duke Lemur Center Paleontologist Matt Borths welcomed guests in the Duke Lemur Center fossil collection and introduced them to lemur-like primates that once lived in Wyoming jungles as well as "The Crystal Skull," a sparkly greater bamboo lemur skull from the northern tip of Madagascar. Attendees learned how paleontologists use fossils to see how environments change and how those changes are linked to extinction.
- Tate Museum celebrated Geologic Map Day by showcasing the many geological maps hanging in their hallways, classrooms, and the break room.
- Buffalo Bill Center of the West, Sheridan College's Geology Museum, and Bighorn Basin Foundation were National Fossil Day partners.
- Tate Geological Museum at Casper College hosted a Facebook Live event for National Fossil Day. Participants learned what the Tate Museum area looked like and which animals lived there during the Permian Period.
- University of Wyoming Geological Museum highlighted a virtual event held with the Tate Geological Museum for National Fossil Day. "Wyoming Rocks: At-Home Activity Kits" were sent to households that submitted a request.
- In honor of National Fossil Day, Wyoming Dinosaur Center highlighted the *Eubostrychoceras matsumoti* fossil, a heteromorph ammonite from the Frontier formation. The public was welcomed at the local natural history museum showing a wide range of fossils found in the world, from small ones like ammonite to the 108-foot *Supersaurus*.
- The Wyoming State Geological Survey and University of Wyoming Geological Museum celebrated with daily activities and fun-fact posts on the survey's social media platforms throughout Earth Science Week.

International Events

According to Google Analytics, the Earth Science Week website was accessed by users in 212 nations, territories, and regions in 2020. Activities worldwide included:

Australia

- Virtual GESSS (Geological Society of Australia Earth Science Student Symposium) was held during Earth Science Week 2020. Participants gave presentations on this year's theme, "Earth Materials in Our Lives."
- To celebrate Earth Science Week 2020, Dr. Jess Stromberg of CSIRO Mineral Resources and Dr. Sima Mousavi of the Australian National University explored the joys, importance, misconceptions, and future of Earth science with an online video series.
- Geoscience Australia's Earth Science Week 2020 celebrated the theme of "Earth Materials in Our Lives."

Bangladesh

- Bangladesh held its third annual Earth Science Week celebration, including photography competitions, an online essay competition, and online seminars.
- Brainex Bangladesh invited and encouraged schools to participate in the four contests of Earth Science Week.
- Daily Samakal Suhrid Samabesh, a leading newspaper in Bangladesh, promoted participation in Earth Science among teachers and citizens.

Belgium

- For the first time in its nearly 20-year history, the Belgian Science Policy Office held a virtual border-crossing Earth Observation Day event this year.

Belize

- Galen University's Anthropology Club hosted a virtual International Archaeology Day celebration. The event included a television show (also streamed on a Facebook page) on the material culture of Belize and the importance of heritage education and stewardship.

Brazil

- AAPG UNICAMP Student Chapter organized a series of three online talks on subjects relating to the Earth Science Week 2020 theme. Talks were offered live on a YouTube channel on October 12, 14, and 16.

Canada

- The Ontario Archaeological Society participated in International Archaeology Day by inviting all members and symposium attendees to participate in its photo contest.
- Alberta's radio station, b93.fm, shared a post in celebration of National Fossil Day.
- The Royal Ontario Museum celebrated International Archaeology Day with a free online video presentation with archaeologist Dr. Craig Cipolla, who talked about his current work and how experimental archaeology helps us understand the past.

Greece

- The Archaeological Museum of Ancient Corinth celebrated International Archaeology Day with a program, "The Archaeological Site, My Backyard," on October 17.

India

- Maharashtra Vruksha Samvardhini and Mission Devrai hosted a lecture series on October 11–18 in celebration of Earth Science Week across India.
- Abhinav Public Senior Secondary School in Delhi held Earth Science Week Udaipur online on October 11–17. Participants offered presentations relating to this year's theme, "Earth Materials in Our Lives."

Ireland

- Earth Science Week events took place in museums, libraries, schools, universities, geoparks, and additional sites. Activities included urban geowalks, family activity days, talks, conservation days, and field trips.
- Earth Science Week Toolkits were distributed to students, teachers, and others by the Mineralogical Society of Great Britain and Ireland.

Italy

- University of Helsinki sponsored a conference at the Royal Academy of Spain in Rome, Italy.

Japan

- The third annual Earth Science Week Japan was celebrated in Shizuoka on October 11–17 at Museum of Natural and Environmental History, Shizuoka.
- Innovinc Organization held the second World Congress on Geology & Earth Science in Osaka, Japan.

Pakistan

- The Save Cultural Heritage Group and its partners organized virtual International Archaeology Day celebrations at Islamabad to share knowledge and experience which foster understanding of challenges and opportunities in the art, architecture and archaeology, and related cultural heritage sectors.

Poland

- "Around the World and Through the Ages with Garb on the Back" was presented at Muzeum Górnośląskie w Bytomiu on October 17.

Portugal

- Earth Science Week 2020 Toolkits were distributed to students, teachers, and others by the Universidade de Aveiro.

Russia

- Along with more than 100 Collaborating Organizations, the Archeological Institute of America promoted celebrations of International Archeology Day in cities around the globe including Samara, Russia.

Spain

- Cuevas del Almanzora celebrated International Archaeology Day with guided visits to Fuente Alamo, one of the most important ancient Argaric Culture sites in the Mediterranean.

Trinidad & Tobago

- The UWI Seismic Research Centre promoted participation in Earth Science Week on its website and through social media with educational posts, videos, and more.

Turkey

- Sri Utami of Pamukkale, Denizli Province, Turkey, was a finalist in the 2020 Earth Science Week video contest.
- An online event, "Past and Future of Turkish Archeology," was hosted in Ankara Turkey in celebration of International Archaeology Day 2020.

United Arab Emirates

- The Sharjah Archaeology Authority organized a large-scale program to mark International Archaeological Day, which included field visits to archaeological sites, media tours, and a virtual lecture.

United Kingdom

- The Geological Society of London (GSL) supported several Earth Science Week events, including geowalks, hands-on activities, talks, and open days.
- GSL also hosted a photography competition for Earth Science Week with the theme "Earth Materials in Our Lives." Winning photos are included in GSL's 2021 calendar.
- Earth Science Week 2020 Toolkits were distributed to students, teachers, and others by the International Association of Hydrogeologists.
- Taylor & Francis Group encouraged people around the world to participate in Earth Science Week by highlighting activities for Focus Days of Earth Science Week on the group's website.

Because of the large and growing number of news items citing Earth Science Week activities and resources, the print edition of the report does not include clippings. To view the hundreds of press releases and news items promoting awareness of Earth Science Week each year, please go online to **www.earthsciweek.org/highlights**. Thank you for helping us in our efforts to conserve resources and protect the environment.